DESIGNING BETTER LIBRARIES

Selecting and Working With Building Professionals

Richard C. McCarthy, A.I.A.

The Highsmith Press Handbook Series

Highsmith PRESS
Fort Atkinson, Wisconsin

laughter, Mary Augusta McCarthy,
ahead of her.

Acknowledgments: I would like to thank the following people who made this book possible:

My wife, Susan Stillinger, for her endless patience and help;

Chuck Cassell, A.I.A., for proofreading the manuscript and offering much good advice;

Jack Stillinger and Tom Stillinger for varied and valuable assistance;

Charles Burnidge A.I.A. and my co-workers at Burnidge Cassell for support and advice and

Miriam Pollack of the North Suburban Library System, whose idea led to the writing of this book.

Published by Highsmith Press
W5527 Highway 106
P.O. Box 800
Fort Atkinson, Wisconsin 53538-0800
1-800-558-2110

© Richard C. McCarthy, 1995
Cover Illustration: Mary Ann Highsmith

The paper used in this publication meets the minimum requirements of American National Standard for Information Science —
Permanence of Paper for Printed Library Material.
ANSI/NISO Z39.48-1992.

Library of Congress Cataloging in Publication

McCarthy, Richard C. (Richard Charles), 1955–
     Designing better libraries : selecting and working with building
professionals / Richard C. McCarthy.
          p.   cm. --(The Highsmith Press handbook series)
     Includes bibliographical references and index.
     ISBN 0-917846-36-2
     1. Library buildings--United States--Design and construction.
I. Title. II. Series.
Z679.2.U54M33   1995
727' .8'0973--dc20   94-40730
                                                                  CIP

Contents

1
A Common Language

In architecture school I was taught many things. I learned how to design buildings, and how to draw. I learned how a structure stands against the force of gravity and resists attacks by the elements. There were courses in plumbing, electrical systems and the mechanical properties of soils. We students spent long nights memorizing slides and photographs of significant buildings for architectural history. There was even a one semester class in office practice, in which the teachers introduced us to the more pragmatic sides of the architectural profession: things like contracts, budgets, liability insurance and bookkeeping. Being young, we mounted a fierce resistance to all things practical and eagerly quit that classroom to return to the design studio where our interests and, we hoped, our talents lay. We spent six years learning the skills and nomenclature of our profession: the art and process of designing buildings.

Architecture is one of the few professions that still requires a period of formal apprenticeship. After receiving a degree, the graduate is required to work at least three years under the tutelage of a licensed architect before he or she can begin the rigorous examination process that is a prerequisite to licensure. In most cases, nine years of a person's life has been devoted to studying the profession before he or she can assume the title of "Architect."

Learning the ropes

Despite its rigors, nothing in our education prepared us to stand up in front of skeptical board members and try to persuade them of the necessity to spend additional money for their project because the contractor's bids were higher than we had anticipated. There was no training to ready us for difficult negotiations with local authorities to obtain a politically unpopular zoning change on behalf of a client. The problem of non-payment for services rendered never came up. As is probably the case with most professions, we learn many of the most important skills of our profession on the job.

The typical member of a library board is usually elected or appointed to the position without the benefit of years of preparation or a formal training period. Learning the ropes is as important for a new board member as it is for a fledgling architect. The new board member finds him or herself suddenly in the position of having to decide and to vote upon issues that may be only partially understood. The first board meetings are filled with acronyms that leave novices in a state of confusion. They can be seen furtively searching the board information packet for anything that will help in translation. Budgets are reviewed and at least a passing acquaintance with accountancy is assumed. Library employees who may have formerly been cool and business-like suddenly seem eager to please. The new member is faced with the unfamiliar and confronted with an overload of information.

In time, the footing becomes more sure. Acronyms begin to assume meaning. With assistance from the more senior members, the neophyte begins to feel that he or she is a part of the group. If the chemistry is right, the board functions as a team, with each member contributing the benefits of his or her own talents and experience. Sometimes, a board will be confronted with a problem that may lie beyond the combined experience of the group. The decision to construct a new building, or to enlarge an existing one, is not one that needs to be made on a regular basis. Often the last such project predates the terms of the current board members and perhaps even that of the library director.

The degree of success of such an enterprise will depend upon decisions made early in the project. Its outcome may have an effect on the community for a generation or more. Public bodies often begin this decision-making process not really speaking the same language as the professionals they are proposing to hire, without having a clear idea of the services they need or even of what services are available. Unfortunately, there are no practice runs, and few manuals to offer guidance. The learning curve is very steep. For the most part you do it once and either things turn out as you hoped, or they fall short of your expectations.

Thousands of buildings are built each year that are of doubtful aesthetic value but still plod along, functioning pretty much as they were intended. Others may sacrifice utility in order to make an artistic point. Neither of these constitutes an unsuccessful project if the clients got what they wanted and understood in advance the limitations of the finished product. The mission of the architect is to produce the most successful building possible while responding to the varied, and sometimes contradictory wishes of the client. It is the unpleasant surprises that can cause dissatisfaction with the final result. To avoid these surprises it is important that the client and architect understand each other's language.

Good architects keep the client fully informed at every step of the project. They spend large amounts of time with the owner, explaining the process and progress of the work. Good clients spend the time that it takes to keep current with the project. When the client is a group of persons rather than an individual, communication becomes more difficult. Often a board of directors will only see the architect during a project report at a monthly board meeting. Other information about the job comes from intermediaries, perhaps the library director or another staff member. In these instances it is important that each member of the decision-making body has a basic understanding of the process. A book cannot keep you informed of the progress of your particular project, but it can give you an overview of how to work with an architect and of the way that buildings are designed, bid and built. Understanding the language and methods of the architect will enable you to communicate more effectively with each other and thus allow you to play an active and essential role in the project.

This book will describe the process of a building project. The point of view that I take is that of an architect. It is tempered by the fact that, as of this writing, I am serving my eighth year as a library trustee. I will try to balance these two roles and present you with as objective a view as is possible. We will look at methods that can be used by library boards and directors to aid them in selecting, hiring and working with architects and other design professionals. I will cover what you can expect from an architect in terms of services, and offer assistance to help you determine what services you may need. Examples of documents and graphic presentations will be offered. Subjects include the parts of a typical architectural project, the evaluation of architectural firms, guidelines for interviewing architects and advice on coping with common problems and procedures during construction. An understanding of the process will boost the chances of a successful project and help insure that you are getting your money's worth for the professional services for which you are paying.

I will not attempt to offer guidelines for designing libraries. There a number of guides in print which propose standards for public libraries. Several of these documents are listed in the bibliographies at the end of this book. Standards such as these should be used by the client, the library building consultant and the architect in arriving at a design solution appropriate to your particular circumstances. I recommend that you examine such materials before beginning a project.

With all the responsibilities of spending the public's money on a complex undertaking, you may feel that the weight of the world is on your shoulders. Take advantage of this opportunity to have some fun! In a well-run project, all participants play a part in the creative effort. The architect will bring focus to the endeavor, but you are in control. This is the time for you to express your hopes and ideas and see them realized in the form of a building. I find that learning about my clients is the most rewarding part of my profession. As an architect, I have a unique opportunity to step into their shoes, to see how they live and work and to help them seek solutions to their problems. For the client, it's a time of self examination. You will learn a lot about yourself and about how your library functions. This is the time for you to step back and take an objective look at how you do things. The opportunity to change the built environment may bring the chance to improve your operations. Encourage staff involvement in this appraisal process and invite their input at every opportunity. There are all sorts of good ideas out there that are just waiting to be heard.

2

First Things First

There are a number of questions you should ask yourself before considering a building project. The first and most obvious question is best summed up by the old World War II poster which aimed to persuade the public to conserve resources by asking the reader "Is *your* trip necessary?" I suspect that most readers have already persuaded themselves that it is, but the issue still merits some thought. Your reasons will have to be put forth in a clear and concise form, both as a basis for internal discussion and to provide justification which may be required by the tax-paying public and other funding sources. Alternatives to new construction should always be considered. When the financial state of the library is less than robust, working within the existing building envelope may be your only option. Some preliminary work is required to be able to make this kind of analysis.

Consider the alternatives

The alternatives to a new building or addition are often far less exciting than the idea of building something new. Remodeling just doesn't capture one's imagination in the same way. An "Excuse our dust!" sign in the lobby can seem like a poor substitute for a newspaper photo of a ground-breaking. If a shortage of square footage is the main problem, stacks, reading tables, card catalogs, etc., can often be rearranged in a more efficient manner to yield more usable

space. An unused basement space might be finished and utilized as a public area. In a real pinch, mobile units may be brought in (on a temporary basis), for storage or staff space. An architect can help you to evaluate these options, and provide you with alternate plans and budget figures. Since the passage of the Americans With Disabilities Act (ADA), some interior improvements will trigger additional required work, sometimes undermining the rationale of these cost-saving alternatives. Program changes can also be considered. Things that the library currently provides that may be considered as "secondary services," like meeting rooms or video collections could be sacrificed to free up space for "primary services." Triage of library services should be reserved for real emergencies, as the results can easily be counterproductive in terms of public opinion.

There are some other considerations that can conspire against the case for remodeling. The current bogey man in the world of building restoration is asbestos. If your building was built before the early 1970s, there is a strong likelihood that it contains many forms of this versatile, and now prohibited, material. In many of its applications, asbestos is a relatively innocuous substance. It resides in boiler rooms and above ceilings, quietly fireproofing structural steel and insulating pipes. It replaced horse hair as an ingredient in plaster. In older floor tiles it is a binder, helping to hold the tiles together to insure a long-wearing floor. Try to alter any of these installations, however, and Pandora's box is opened. You no doubt already know that disturbing asbestos can release large numbers of the carcinogenic fibers into the air, this is prohibited by federal law. The legal alternative is often to release large sums of your money into the pocket of an asbestos abatement contractor. Removing asbestos can be very expensive. Costs for the management of asbestos and other potential environmental issues should always be researched and considered in a remodeling project.

Having a historically significant building for your library can be a mixed blessing if alterations are being considered. Structures on the National Register of Historic Buildings are protected by state and federal regulations which limit the kinds of alternations which may be made. Most states have a central office for the National Register. You or your architect should contact this office before contemplating any changes to a listed building.

Whether or not you can sell the concept of remodeling or of new construction to those who will eventually foot the bill will depend on how well they understand the need for the work. This seems obvious, and indeed it is. Every year however, referenda are lost, grants are rejected and city councils unpersuaded because someone didn't prepare the way. Communicating the necessity for the work is vitally important.

Some of the reasons that have made you consider building are evident to the public, and some are not. Even a severe shortage of space, one of the most basic reasons for a construction project, may not be apparent to the average library user. People don't expect to see a lot of empty space on library shelves. They may take some note when the books are jammed together so tightly that they become difficult to remove, but they probably won't notice that the collection is being severely weeded just to make room for even a minimum number of new acquisitions.

The sitting areas may have steadily shrunk before the glacial advance of the stacks, but most people probably still get a seat. Patrons seldom get to see the staff areas. Cataloging and shelving rooms may have books stacked several feet high on every horizontal surface and there may be eight staffers crammed in a room designed for four, but to the average visitor all seems well.

Aged and inefficient mechanical systems coupled with inadequate building insulation may result in high utility bills, but few beyond the board and the bookkeeper will know of them. Your present building, especially if it's an older one, may not be accessible to the handicapped. If not, changes are mandated by the Americans With Disabilities Act. In a multi-story structure these changes can become costly. If the building already possesses a number of other inherent shortcomings, the extent of the work required to bring it in conformance with ADA can be significant.

State your case

Making the public aware of your needs is a challenge and will be an important part of any fund-raising effort. District libraries often depend upon referenda for capital improvements. This usually means that the library director and board members hit the local lecture circuit. They can be seen stumping for the library, competing with rubber chicken and rice pilaf for the attention of noon hour Rotarians. On an appointed board it may be possible to select a member or two based primarily on their public image and speaking abilities. In times of financial need, this can be a good investment.

Some shortcomings are more obvious to the public, and are a much easier sell. Parking can represent a real problem. It's an unfortunate fact that in our society people are unaccustomed to walking. Public libraries tend to be located in older, established areas, often downtown. Many downtown plans predate the age of the automobile and parking can be scarce, inconveniencing those who must drive to the library. A deteriorating neighborhood, another common condition in a downtown area, may cause people to want the library relocated to a "safer" part of town. Basing a decision to move on this reasoning can have important political considerations as a public library may be the last, best hope for revitalizing a distressed area. There may be a public demand for more amenities such as meeting rooms, or other space for scheduled events. Expanding children's services can be a popular move as well as the addition of special collections. At our local library, one of the most popular areas is the genealogy collection. Making this resource available to the public generates more support for funding efforts than any amount of crying about leaking roofs, old boilers and worn-out carpet.

Sometimes a structure suffices for the present but falls short when the projection of future needs is taken into account. If the building site is fully utilized and some adjacent property becomes available, it may result in a "now or never" decision, always an uncomfortable position. Persuading someone to spend money based on anticipation of future needs can be difficult. Some libraries have found it helpful to retain a specialized referendum consultant to direct and lend credence to their efforts.

Your team

Your in-house team is just as important as the team that will eventually be assembled by the architect. An important first step to any project is defining which board and staff members will work most closely with the architect. From the earliest stages of a project, a library should have a building committee to coordinate the efforts of the board and staff. A well-balanced building committee might be made up a several board members, the library director and several staff members. There are two general types of tasks that the group will be called upon to do. In the earliest stages of the project, information-gathering will be the primary goal. The general focus for this effort may be set by a building consultant or the architect, but the responsibility for the collection of the information will often rest with the staff. Later on, decision-making becomes more important. At this stage the board members bear the ultimate responsibility as many of the decisions involve money, and must be voted on by the board. The library staff, however, plays a vital advisory role to the board at this time. Few board members can make a full-time commitment to the project and thus depend upon the director and the staff to function as their eyes and ears.

Having several of your board members sit on a building committee and make their reports to the full board has several advantages. Of course, the first is time. Building projects can require lots of additional meetings beyond the usual monthly board session. Not all of the members of the board may be able to make the commitment for the additional time that will be required. More importantly, when the building committee makes its reports to the full board, the remainder of the board members function as an important check on the recommendations made by the committee. Decisions of any importance are always best reviewed with fresh insight.

It makes sense to have the director and several department heads represent the staff on a committee. Other staff members with appropriate talents should also be considered. A lot of information will be funneled through these individuals, and people with good listening and organizational skills are always assets to the committee. Management skills are also a plus. Good internal management will help maintain a smooth flow of information to the design professionals and will help you make efficient use of the resources that you are paying for. Teamwork is the most essential ingredient of the mixture and is essential in a successful project.

A house divided

Lastly, is the project supported by the entire board? At this early stage it may be more appropriate to say, "Is the *concept* of the project supported by the entire board?" Until now, the project has been defined in only the broadest of terms. The design isn't fixed and costs are only the roughest of approximations. Within this framework, however, it is important that there is a consensus regarding the need for the work.

A library building consultant can play an important role in bringing a board together. Some states mandate the use of a library building consultant for projects over a specified minimum cost. The consultant will make an in-depth study of your current facility and compare it against present and projected needs. Having the consultant confirm what the library director has been saying regarding the inadequacies of the current library can help to persuade any undecided board members. It will also give the rest of the board a greater level of comfort. The building consultant will not design the new building or addition, but he or she will be able to give you an idea of the approximate number of square feet that will be required. It is an easy matter to apply the square footage to the average cost of construction in your area and get a rough estimate of the potential cost of the building. When doing this, it is important to be sure that the costs of site work, furnishings and the costs of alterations to the existing structure are taken into account. They can add a hefty and sometimes unexpected surcharge to the cost of a building. After the library consultant's report is completed, an architect could be brought in on a preliminary basis to help the board analyze the feasibility of the proposed project. He or she might be retained at this point to do a feasibility study with no guarantee of getting the rest of the potential project. A feasibility study would also add to the comfort level within the board. These architectural services will be discussed in more detail later.

These discussions have assumed that objections to expansion of the library are based on the state of the library's finances. There are a number of other possible reasons that one or several board members may not support a large capital project. There may be differences in philosophy regarding the role of the library in the community. A member may object to the library providing services that he or she doesn't see as falling within the "traditional" role of a library (video and recorded book collections, meeting rooms, public use computers, specialized children's libraries). An elected member on a district board may have run on a "No new taxes!" platform, or just have a very conservative stand on the expenditure of public money for any but the most urgent needs. The best answer for these dilemmas may involve educating the board on the range of services that modern libraries offer. Even the most fiscally conservative people can usually be convinced that a library is an investment in the future of their community.

I first ran for our local library board because I love libraries, not because I had any profound understanding of their problems or particular insight into the role they play in our society. Over time, I gained a deeper appreciation of what they can offer and of the challenges facing them in these times of tight money. I believe that the more a person knows about libraries the more he or she is likely to support improvements of all types. Local library systems and state library associations provide many avenues for trustee education. Urge new board members to explore some of these opportunities. Consensus comes more easily to an informed board.

The longest journey begins with a single step

That first step is an important one; if taken with assurance and planning, it can fix the direction and pace for the largest of projects. If tentative and unprepared, it may set a precedent for indecision. For a library board considering a construction project, the first step is the definition of a goal. Without a goal we cannot define a project, or if need be, defend it. Do you wish merely to reflect the community's growth with proportional expansion at the library? Is the aim to provide a wider range of services to the public, or to enhance certain aspects that might complement those of other local libraries? Do you wish to expand all departments equally, or is the aim to develop an appeal to a special group of library users—say business people or children? To define your goals, such questions must be considered and decisions formally adopted. The library director, with his or her professional background in library science, should be the driving force behind the formulation of the goals. For a library, the goals can be stated in the form of a five, ten or twenty-year plan. This plan is your first step.

The development of a long range plan is not within the scope of this book. It should be an ongoing process at every library. If you feel that your institution lacks a solid long-term plan, or if the existing one is out of date, the development of one should be made a priority. Your state library and local library system can supply you with materials to assist you in your planning efforts.

The library building consultant

With a long-term plan in hand you are in a position to consider hiring a consultant who will analyze your needs and interpret them in terms of what will be required to satisfy those needs. That consultant may be either an architect or library building consultant. As mentioned earlier, some states require you to use a library building consultant for projects over a specified size to qualify for public money. The requirement will vary so you should seek the opinion of your legal counsel before committing to a course of action.

The scope of services of a library building consultant overlaps somewhat with the scope of services traditionally offered by an architect.

There are, however, a number of advantages in beginning with a library building consultant rather than an architect. Several of them are:

1. Library building consultants often come from a library background. Some are library directors. In the first chapter of this book we discussed the need for a common language. The library building consultant arrives on the scene already fluent in the language of the library professional, which can help to ease the slope of that learning curve. This is especially useful if there is a possibility that the architect you will eventually select may not have a lot of experience in library design.

2. Following on the above, the use of a library building consultant may open up the field of architects that you consider for your project, allowing you to expand your options. The program developed by the library building consultant would be a uniform point of beginning for any architect's efforts.

3. Drawing upon a larger base of library experience, the library building consultant may be better able to anticipate problems and opportunities particular to the library environment.

4. The library building consultant will probably have a better grasp than an architect on specialized sources of funding for libraries.

5. Retaining a library building consultant can lend credibility to the planning effort. Political realities may demand that advice regarding the expenditure of public money come from a "disinterested" source. If the library building consultant has no vested interest in the outcome of the planning process, he or she can fill the role of that disinterested third party.

A final note, as the program developed by the library building consultant replaces, to a degree, that which would have been put together by an architect, there could be a proportional decrease in the architectural fees. The savings may not be on an equal basis, as the architect still must refine the building program, but they could at least partially offset the cost of the library building consultant's services.

What should you expect from your library building consultant?

In short, a library building consultant will produce a building program. We will discuss just what a building program should include in chapter five where the parts of a building project will be covered in detail. For the moment, suffice it to say that a building program defines each architectural space in the proposed building. Each space is assigned an approximate square footage. Furniture and equipment requirements are itemized and how the room must relate to the other spaces around it is discussed. The square footage figures can be used to get your first intimation of the potential cost of your project. Note that the library building consultant's report does not generally take financial considerations into account. His or her mission is to assess needs independent of the means required to meet those needs.

> *If you have to ask, you can't afford it.*
> **J. P. Morgan**

Money. How much do you have? How much do you spend? How much are you going to have? How much are you going to need? Unfortunately, we do have to ask, but in spite of Mr. Morgan's classic quote, maybe you can afford it. The real question is *how* to afford it. These questions will play an important role in the planning process. Having an expert third party evaluation of your current financial state and prospects for the future, is an important component of a long range plan. When seeking additional funding for your institution, be it by grant, appropriation or referendum, this kind of expert opinion is advised, and may be mandatory. There is (not surprisingly), another consultant in the line-up who specializes in providing just these kinds of evaluations.

The financial planning consultant

Back to that "Longest Journey." You know that you're going somewhere—your long-term plan tells you that much. Based on research and work with library personnel, your library building consultant has told you where you should be going. Two additional players, the financial planning consultant and the architect, will give you advice on how to get there. We will first talk about the role of the financial planning consultant in this process. When the library building consultant has completed the building program, his or her report gives you an idea on the size, and hence the cost of your potential project. At this point you are ready to begin talking to a financial planning consultant. This consultant can assist you in three general areas.

The financial plan

The first is the formulation of a financial plan. This plan is a necessary companion to your long range plan. The financial plan will take into account all aspects of the library's present and anticipated financial condition. Like the long range plan, the financial plan may be written with a ten to twenty year time horizon. After anticipated revenue is compared with projected expenditures, inflation is added to the mixture and a projection of the long-term financial condition of the library emerges. Many of these numbers are necessarily based on educated guesses. Projecting the library's income requires prognosticating future tax rates, grants and changes in assessed valuation. An accurate estimate of future expenses requires that the crystal ball be tuned to the rate of inflation and general trends in library services, with a healthy amount thrown in to cover the unexpected. It would be an interesting exercise for example, to look at some 20-year-old financial plans and see if any of them correctly predicted the costs of the computers that play such large roles in today's libraries.

Like the library building consultant, the financial planning consultant will work closely with the library director in formulating his or her evaluations. The board will most likely be only peripherally involved until the presentation of the financial plan. When the report is presented it will give solid information on the means and methods by which to implement the long-term plan, including proposed changes or additions to the library. The report will establish the tax rates required to implement your plans, show you whether or not a referendum will be required, and if so, can specify the types of questions that will need to be on the ballot. In the case of libraries that aren't fueled by tax dollars, it can instruct you on the amounts and possible sources of the funding that you will require.

Taking it to the voters

Referenda are unpredictable. Like children, no two of them are alike. Strategies that might bring success in one situation may flop in another. The average board member probably has little experience in launching a referendum. It therefore makes sense to take advantage of any expertise at your disposal for such an important effort. Many financial planning consultants can also offer assistance with your referendum. The amount of help that they can provide will vary widely depending on your needs and your in-house abilities.

The financial planning consultant can offer assistance on many aspects of running a referendum. He or she might help you in determining your overall strategy for your campaign, or assist in any of a hundred small details that can make the difference between winning and losing. Techniques for informing the voters, election timing, coordination of publicity and the formulation of citizens' committees might be included. A strong citizens' committee will add many voices to your cause and be an important facet of your referendum; the more voters that are involved, the better your chances of success. The right financial planning consultant can show you ways to promote a strong public involvement in your effort.

In addition to the financial planning consultant, your state library and local library system can be important sources of help and information. They often have collections of referenda materials distributed by other libraries in your state and records of past voting results that you can use in your planning.

Following a successful referendum, the financial planner will direct the sale and marketing of general obligation library bonds or mortgage notes. He or she will determine the timing of the sale, set the terms or recommend taking bids for the bond registrar, printer and counsel. Finally, the consultant will recommend that the sale be either negotiated or competitively bid.

After the above decisions are made, he or she will write a prospectus for review by potential investors. General obligation bonds for libraries are usually considered attractive investments and are often sold at favorable rates. To boost the attraction of the bonds, the consultant may recommend that the library secure a bond rating from Moody's Investor Service or Standard and Poors. The library board should be kept informed of the actions of the financial consultant, as should the library's legal counsel.

Note that it can take up to two years from the time that you begin planning your referendum to the time when the money starts rolling in. Add another year or two to complete a building project. This lead time must always be considered in your intermediate and long-term planning.

Experts, experts everywhere... finding library consultants

Finding the right consultant for you will take some homework. In searching for consultants, begin with your state library and library system, some of which will keep lists of qualified individuals. Call other libraries in your area that have passed referenda and/or recently completed a building project. You will probably find that some of the same names keep turning up as the field isn't very large. It should be relatively easy to arrive at a list of persons to interview. Two publications listed in the bibliography can help you in interviewing and hiring library consultants; *Selecting Library Consultants* by Richard Finn and James R. Johnston, and *Building a New Library* by Anthony J. Batco and Richard E. Thompson. These publications are published by the Illinois Library Association as part of its "Trustee Facts File," a collection of articles devoted to the education of library trustees. Contact your state library association to see if it publishes similar materials.

3

When to Use an Architect

Architecture is the art of how to waste space. **Philip Johnson**

Mr. Johnson is a world famous architect and noted writer of architectural theory. I am therefore ill-qualified to comment on his summation of our mutual profession. In spite of this, I will say that I suspect that it would be a grave marketing error to describe oneself as an accomplished waster of space. I also feel obliged to add a few items to his version of our job description. The real question is, what can an architect do for you? In this age of the specialist, most architects still regard themselves as generalists, and customarily offer a wide range of services that address nearly anything that involves a building or a site. They are accustomed to familiarizing themselves with the characteristics of many different types of buildings. In chapter twelve we will discuss whether or not it is important to hire an architect with a lot of experience in designing libraries.

When to use an architect

Most people envision an architect as the designer of buildings. They may have mental images of presentations of impressively rendered illustrations. The renderings invariably show sunlight slanting across broad plazas, trees in midsummer foliage perfectly framing the proposed building. Detailed models and grand plans drawn on large sheets of tracing paper may come to mind. These images do reflect the practice of architecture, but only a small part of it. Many of the services and products that the architect will provide are a lot less exciting than those sunlit plazas, but they are just as important.

Those other services include assisting you with such things as reroofing, recarpeting and other maintenance projects. They will encompass ADA evaluations, energy efficiency studies, interior design, furniture selection, signage consultation, landscape design and assistance with grant applications. Sometimes the need for an architect may be questioned. A lot of your projects will not require the assistance of an architect, but some will benefit by having one to coordinate the work. Let's study an example that illustrates the rationale for utilizing an architect.

High and dry

We'll take a re-roofing project. First, let's establish the scene. You head the building committee of the Roosevelt Library District. The current roof on the library is over 20 years old. It's what is called a "built-up" roof, made up of layers of asphalt-impregnated fabric topped with gravel. It has given good service over the years with only a minimum of problems. Recently however, more and more leaks have been appearing. Your building engineer, armed with large buckets of black, sticky roofing compound, has been making frequent trips up top to make repairs. In spite of her efforts, after every hard rain the staff report more stained ceiling tiles revealing the presence of new leaks. It's clearly time to do something about the situation. Your library director wisely anticipated the problem in the long-term financial plan and in this year's budget there is a $30,000 line item intended to cover the cost of a new roof. Most states require that public projects with an anticipated cost of over a few thousand dollars must be competitively bid. Your office manager has therefore had a notice printed in the local paper stating that bids for a new roof will be received at the library. It also specifies that the bids are to be delivered by one p.m. on the first of April and will be publicly opened immediately afterward. Prospective bidders can be seen on the roof, pacing off distances, inspecting flashings and taking core samples to test for insulation that has been saturated with water. In the mean time, the increased foot traffic on the roof has caused even more leaks to appear and the staff is placing plastic sheets over the computers every night in case of rain.

April first arrives and by one o'clock four bids have arrived. The bidders are sitting in the conference room awaiting the opening. An additional bid is delivered at five minutes after the hour, the contractor explains that one of the bridges in town is closed and that traffic is moving very slowly. Your office manager rejects the late bid, citing the one o'clock stipulation in the advertisement for bids. The roofer storms out, shouting that the advertisement never stated that late bids would be rejected and that you just might hear from his lawyer and that he's a taxpayer too, and that he helped raise money during the last referendum and that the other bidders aren't local anyway... The library director and several board members arrive, (a little late due to traffic tie-ups), and soon everyone is ready to open the bids. The office manager opens the first envelope, and reads:

The A.B.C. Roofing Company is pleased to submit this bid for a new built-up roof for the Roosevelt Library.

Bid includes:

Tear-off of existing roofing and installation of new built-up roofing. Disposal of waste material to be via dumpsters supplied by the library district. Work to be accomplished within 60 days of receipt of signed proposal.

Total installed cost: $25,000

Signed; *[signature]*

President A.B.C. Roofing Inc.

The representative from A.B.C. Roofing nods, "Built up roofing, asphalt, felt and gravel. Been around for 100 years and it's still the best there is!" This doesn't sound too bad, it's the same kind of roof that the library has had, your building engineer knows how to maintain it (you can see her in the back row nodding her agreement), and it costs less than the $30,000 that you have set aside for the job. The office manager opens the second bid and reads it.

The Ever-Dry Roofing Company is pleased to submit this bid for a new E.P.D.M. roof for the Roosevelt Library.

Bid includes:

Tear-off of existing roofing and insulation. Install new E.P.D.M. roofing membrane over new tapered insulation. Disposal of waste materials off-site. Repair of damaged flashing at north side of roof top mechanical unit. Work to be accomplished within 90 days of receipt of signed proposal.

Total installed cost: $35,000.00

All work covered under manufacturer's 20 year warrantee.

Signed; *[signature]*

President, Ever-Dry Roofing Ltd.

- Fully insured
- State Roofers License # 234-778

It's definitely more expensive than the first bid but they are including more, aren't they? The

Ever-Dry man is in the audience. "E.P.D.M. is the state of the art in roofing membranes, a spin-off from the space program. It'll last a lot longer than those antique built-up systems." His tone reminds you of a recent convert to a fringe religious group, but he does have you wondering if the additional work that he included might not be a good idea.

The third bid is read.

Bob's Roofing and Bait Shop is pleased to submit this bid for a new roof for the Roosevelt Library.

Bid includes: Replacement of existing roof. (New roof to match existing.)

Total cost: $12,750.00

Signed; *Bob*

President, Bob's Roofing and Bait Shop

It's the low bid so far. Do you have to accept it even if it looks a little, well... unprofessional? Bob is in the audience. He's shifting back and forth in his seat, looking a little nervous. Maybe he's wondering if he missed something. The final bid is opened.

Best Roofing Company is pleased to submit this bid for a new E.P.D.M. roof for the Roosevelt Memorial Library District.

Bid includes:

Tear-off of existing roofing and insulation. Installation of new E.P.D.M. roofing membrane over new tapered insulation. Disposal of waste materials off-site. Repair of damaged flashing at North side of roof top mechanical unit. Work to be accomplished within 90 days of receipt of signed proposal.

Total installed cost: $50,000.00

All work covered under manufacturer's 20 year warrantee.

Signed; *Joe Best*

President, Best Roofing Inc.

-Fully insured and bonded
"Serving Yourtown Since 1946"
State Roofers License # 554-626

This looks like a quality outfit, and at this price they had better be. Isn't the scope of work in this bid a lot like the second one though? Why are the prices so different? This one is almost half again as much as Ever-Dry's price for what seems to be the same work. Something's not right here. The office manager clears her throat. "We will announce the selection of the roofing contractor at the board meeting next Tuesday night. "Thank you for coming."

The building committee is scheduled to meet the day before the regular board meeting to evaluate the bids and arrive at their recommendation. As chair of the committee, you are expected to provide some leadership in the decision making process, but where to start? The first bid was about what you expected and you felt good about it, at least until the second bid was opened. Then, the first in a series of uncomfortable questions began to crop up. You decide to write them down so you can address them one at a time. The list looks something like the following:

1. What is E.P.D.M., and the Space Agency notwithstanding, is it any better than built-up roofing?

2. What about the additional work that Ever-Dry has included on their bid? Do we need new insulation or can the existing material be left on the roof?

3. What about the damaged flashing, is it something that A.B.C. would have included as a part of their work?

4. Is A.B.C.'s work guaranteed, and how much will it cost us to provide the dumpsters? Will a landfill accept the waste material?

5. Do we have to accept Bob's bid as legitimate? If so, are we legally obligated to take the lowest bid?

6. Some say that they are insured. Some that they are bonded. Some say both, and some neither. How do we establish our minimum requirements?

7. Why are some of the bids for the same work so different? Do some of them misunderstand the scope of the work?

8. Bob's Roofing isn't a union shop. Do they have to be union in order to bid public work?

9. After we make the selection and the work begins, how do we know that we are getting what we paid for?

10. And what about that guy with the late bid, could he really sue us?

At this point you realize that this could go on for a long time with no real resolution. The most important question hasn't even been asked yet.

11. Which one do we recommend?

You might feel that you'd be going out on a limb by making any choice based on what you currently know. There's no real way to compare the bids meaningfully. You were proud when they asked you to head the building committee, but now it doesn't seem like such an enviable position.

The role of the architect

Even the seemingly straightforward task of getting a new roof can create a surprising number of complications. In our story you could substitute recarpeting, apparently minor ADA work or even some interior remodeling for the re-roofing project, and exactly the same problems might have arisen. If you can be held accountable for the money that you are spending, you owe it to yourself to insure that all your decisions are based on informed, if not expert, opinion. This is where the concept of "expert insurance" applies.

Hiring a consultant may not only get you a better product, but it can also insulate you from certain questions of liability. The role (and the goal) of the architect is to circumvent the kind of problems that you, as the head of the building committee, were faced with in the fictional re-roofing project. A well-written advertisement for bids, backed with some drawings and a written specification would have prevented most, if not all of the difficulties. Except in cases where the law may require the use of a licensed architect or engineer, (like building a new building or adding an addition) the decision of when to use an architect will rest with the board. In cases like the re-roofing project the use of an architect may not mandatory, but in light of the possible difficulties it may be advisable to hire one. For such projects it will always be something of a judgment call. The best one can do is to weigh the in-house expertise available against the potential risks and see

where the balance lies. Let's summarize some of the advantages of retaining an architect.

1. The architect will produce drawings and specifications that will set minimum standards of quality for the project.

2. The bids that you receive will be more meaningful. It will reduce the chance of having to compare "apples and oranges."

3. You will receive advice on the selection of materials and systems that are appropriate for your project.

4. The architect will work to see that you receive the protection of manufacturer's warrantees and contractor's guarantees of which you otherwise might not be aware.

5. If you wish, the architect can observe the work to confirm that it is being done correctly and in conformance with specifications; and you only approve payments to the contractor after the architect has verified the completion and adequacy of the work.

6. Some products have federal and/or state standards that limit their use in certain locations due to excessive flammability or other safety concerns. An architect's specifications should prohibit the use of such materials in the work.

7. Using an architect will insure that you have adequate records of work done. Old drawings and specifications are invaluable when you are considering an addition or remodeling.

These services will be discussed in detail in the next chapter where we will begin to describe the parts of a typical building project. Although I have been speaking only of architects, the same reasoning applies to other professionals as well. New boilers will require the services of a mechanical engineer; revisions to the building's electrical power system, an electrical engineer; sagging floors require a structural engineer and so on. Some projects require numerous trades. One of the prime duties of the architect is to retain and coordinate the efforts of many different consultants. In addition to structural, mechanical and electrical engineers, a project team may include civil engineers, acoustical engineers, plumbing engineers, landscape architects, building code consultants and others. The architect usually retains the other consultants, and the board is thus spared the responsibility of having to investigate the qualifications and costs of what may be a large number of players. The responsibility of insuring that these diverse groups perform as intended also rests with the architect. For these complicated projects an architect offers what amounts to a "one-stop shopping" service. The architect provides the owner with a single line of communication in place of what might otherwise be a confusing din of contractors, each demanding attention to help deal with his or her own problems.

The architect as agent

During the course of a project the architect acts on behalf of the owner. This leads us to the special nature of the relationship between you and your architect. Your contract with the architect enables the architect to act as your agent. In the simplest sense, agency is the concept that two parties, the owner and the architect, can have a relationship that enables an outside, third party to accept the actions of the agent (the architect) as being binding on the principal (the owner). The legal ramifications of agency can be complex, and it is vital that the board understands just what the architect is empowered to do in its name. When signing a contract with an architect or other professional, it is a good idea to meet with your legal counsel and have him or her advise you on the terms of the contract. Your counsel should give you an explanation in plain language of what actions the architect is empowered to take on your behalf. Standard architectural contracts are often modified to conform to the requirements of a particular project. Your counsel will advise you if any changes should be made to suit your own situation.

The architect as judge

There is one interesting twist in the standard contract. According to the Standard Form of Agreement Between Owner and Architect as published by the American Institute of Architects (AIA), there are situations in which the architect can be required to act as an impartial third party. This is particularly true when the architect must render an interpretation of the contract documents. According to the contract, when making such an interpretation the architect shall "...endeavor to secure faithful performance by both the Owner and the Contractor, shall not show partiality to either, and shall not be liable for the result of any interpretation or decision rendered in good faith in such capacity."[1] Though the architect is working for the client, the architect can not force the contractor to perform any service that is not reasonably inferable in the contract documents. This protects the contractor from arbitrary or capricious actions on the part of the client and is important in maintaining a productive and fair owner/contractor relationship.

The American Institute of Architects

The American Institute of Architects is a nationwide organization of architects, interns and others involved with the practice of architecture. The organization is dedicated to advancing the profession of architecture, enhancing the professional growth of its members and informing the public of the profession. Not every licensed architect will have "A.I.A." after his or her name. Membership in the AIA is strictly voluntary, though the majority of licensed architects do belong to the organization. The AIA publishes a code of ethics for professional conduct which is intended to set basic standards of professional responsibilities.[2] Although the code is not legally binding, it is widely recognized by the profession. The legal responsibilities of the architect are determined by the licensing statutes of each state. The licensing statutes are more general than the AIA ethical standards and are typically intended to protect the health, safety and welfare of the public.

In the next chapter, we shall begin to explore the parts of a typical building project, and look at the roles played by the owner and the architect. Understanding the parts of a project and how they all fit together is the first "vocabulary lesson" in learning to speak the language of the architect.

Notes

1. American Institute of Architects. A.I.A. Document B161a. Washington, DC: The Institute, undated. Part 1.2.10.

2. *The Architect's Handbook of Professional Practice*. Washington, DC: American Institute of Architects, 1988. Section 1.5.

4

Anatomy of a Project

We shall now look at the parts of an architectural project. A contract for complete architectural services can be broken up into as many as nine different phases. Like projects, each contract is unique, and the number of phases that apply to your project will vary. It is important that you, as a potential client, have an understanding of the significance of each part and of how it relates to the project as a whole. To get the maximum benefit from your architect you should know in advance what should be happening during each phase. You should know what you can expect from the architect, and what your architect can expect from you.

In each of the upcoming sections, we will discuss services that the architect might provide as a part of each phase of the project. Some of these services are defined a "basic services" and will usually be included as a part your contract with the architect. Beyond the basic services are the "additional services" which are services that are usually *not* included in the standard AIA contract. Fees for additional services are usually negotiated separately with the architect and are in addition to the fees for basic services. Lists of basic services that you can expect the architect to provide as part of the basic services package are provided in each of the chapters. These lists will give you a quick reference guide to the kinds of services that the architect should be providing. Lists of additional services will also be offered. The additional services

lists will help to illustrate other potential services that your architect can provide should they apply to your project.

Milestones and millstones

The end of each phase represents an identifiable "milestone" in the course of a project, it is also a time when the architect may send you a bill for services rendered during that phase. Meetings should be scheduled with the architect at these points to insure that the entire board is following the course of the project. These meetings also allow you to verify that the architect is producing the product for which you are paying. It is advisable that the board "sign-off" on the project at the end of each phase. There a several reasons for this. A formal sign-off on the project to date can help push members of the board to spend the time to really understand what has been done and the direction in which the project is going. Another reason for the sign-off is to protect the architect. If the board should change its mind about some aspect of the project after they have signed-off on the work, the architect could justifiably ask for additional fees for redesign. The formal sign-off will also help to reduce the chance of misunderstandings regarding the scope of the work and potential requests for additional fees.

Keeping up with a complex project can be a time-consuming task, but it is a mandatory one for those who carry the public trust and spend the public's money. Sticking with it and doing a thorough job at each milestone point is the best way to keep current with your project. As you will often be called upon to make decisions regarding the work, you should have a thorough understanding of the state of your project at all times. Spending the time as it's required will keep you informed of the progress and prevent those milestones from becoming millstones.

5
Programming

Well begun is half done.
Aristotle

Where is the wisdom that we have lost in knowledge? Where is the knowledge that we have lost in information? **T. S. Eliot**

T.S. Eliot might well have been speaking of the information age. We are overwhelmed with information, some of it is useful to us—the larger part of it, however, blends into a data-laden noise that we of the twentieth century have grown adept at tuning out. In the simplest sense, *Architectural Programming* is the process of collecting data, sorting out that which is relevant to the current project and using it as a basis for design. That is a rather dry definition for what can be a satisfying and enjoyable experience.

Programming is also the most interactive phase of an architectural project. For the future users of the building it is a time of both self-expression and self-examination, as they look at themselves and try to identify their needs, desires and dreams. To insure the right information is collected in an efficient way, a formalized procedure for collecting data should be established between the programmer and the client.

A building program can be produced by either a library building consultant, a professional programmer or an architect. For most types of projects, architects tend to do their own programming. In the case of libraries, however, it is often done by a library building consultant. This depends partly on the requirements of your state library. In some states the participation of a library building consultant is required to qualify for state grant money. When a library building consultant is used, the architect will use the library consultant's report as a beginning point and then expand upon it in producing the architectural program. For the sake of simplicity, in this chapter I shall refer to the architect as the programmer. Whether it is done by an architect, a professional programmer or a library building consultant, programming is the essential first step in the design process.

As programming is sometimes done by someone other than the architect, it is not included as a "basic" service in the most popular Owner/Architect Agreement published by the American Institute of Architects.[1] Programming and site analysis are termed "pre-design" services. If you are using this contract, the cost of services for programming and site analysis will be negotiated separately under the heading of "additional services."

What is a building program?

A completed building program will usually be in the form of a written document. Sometimes it is primarily text; sometimes it will have accompanying diagrams. The program sets out the special requirements for the building. These requirements are established through research and interviews with people who will use the building. The following includes some of the most important information that your building program should address.

General statement of goals: The goals for the building should be stated. This is especially important as it is a verification that the architect, the users and the board of directors all have the same expectations for what the building should be and how the building should work.

Spatial requirements: The building program should define each significant room in the planned structure, as well as exterior spaces that play an important role in the function of the building. The area in square feet for each space should be given as should the ceiling height.

Adjacencies and room relationships: Adjacency requirements describe how each space is to relate to the other spaces around it. There are a number of ways that rooms can relate to each other. Some situations may require good visual communication from one room to the other. Other times, the rooms may need to be visually or acoustically isolated. One room might require easy access to one of it's neighbors and need to be completely separated from another. Sometimes rooms must be placed in close proximity to each other; sometimes they must be separated by as much distance as possible. Adjacency requirements can be expressed in written form, by using matrices or with graphics.

An adjacency matrix is usually generated before a bubble diagram. In it, the name of each significant room or space in the proposed building is listed on each row and each column of a grid. The names for each of the rooms will thus cross somewhere on the matrix. At this intersection, a symbol indicates the nature of the relationship between the two rooms. After the adjacency matrix is complete, the architect can begin to prepare a bubble diagram. While it is not a floor plan, a bubble diagram goes one step beyond an adjacency matrix by indicating something about the path that one must take to get to a particular space. As an example, an adjacency matrix would indicate that the lobby

and the entry vestibule were related to one another and needed to be placed in close proximity. It would take a bubble diagram however, to tell you that you could only get to the lobby by going *through* the vestibule. (*See samples of an adjacency matrix and bubble diagram on next two pages.*)

Room amenities: The program should give detailed information about other features that have been requested by the client, these will include things such as number and sizes of windows, interior finishes, casework, closets and lighting requirements.

Mechanical, electrical and plumbing: Special requirements for mechanical, electrical and plumbing (M.E.P.) systems should be given. Special electrical and cooling provisions for a computer room would be an example, as would a filtered air system for a hospital operating room. A typical library staff room may have a number of items that would fit in this category, including a sink, water supply and drain connections for a refrigerator ice-maker, a 220-volt electrical supply for an electric oven, a telephone jack and a public address system speaker. A lot of items that come under the M.E.P. classification are things that are either hidden out of sight or that one tends to take for granted. Your architect can help you to identify your requirements.

Furnishings: Often building programs will include information regarding furnishings. The selection of furniture and other furnishings is termed an "additional service" in the Standard Owner/Architect Agreement and is often not included as a part of the architect's scope of work. Even when he or she will not be selecting the furnishings, information regarding anticipated furnishings is usually collected by the architect as a aid in determining the required dimensions for each space. The information tabulated in the program can be a valuable resource for the user in establishing the amount of additional furniture that must be purchased.

One other "furnishing" also deserves mention: art. A commitment could be made at this time to include original art as a part of your building. Original artwork can take many forms in a building project. Paintings, murals or sculpture in the lobby come to mind immediately but there are other, less orthodox forms it can take. Some very successful bas-relief forms have

Adjacency Matrix

Roosevelt Public Library

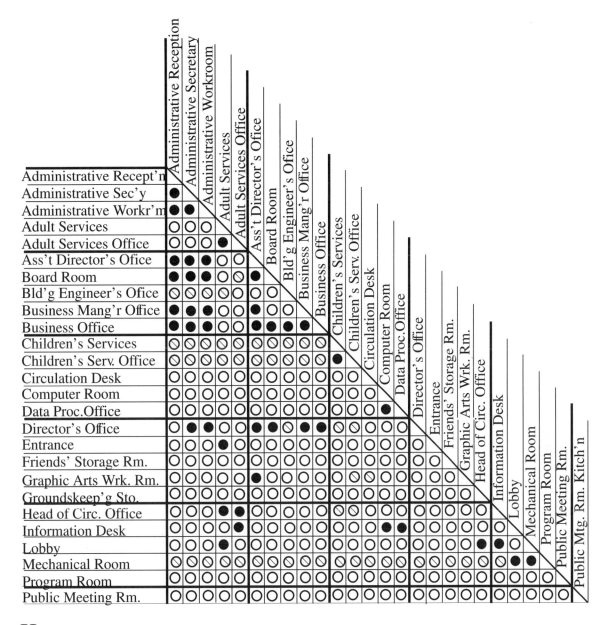

Key:
- ● Positive Adjacency — Spaces are directly related
- ○ Neutral Adjacency — Spaces share no common relationship
- ◐ Negative Adjacency — Spaces should be separated

BUSSARD, STEVER & TOTES - ARCHITECTS

Bubble Diagram
Roosevelt Public Library

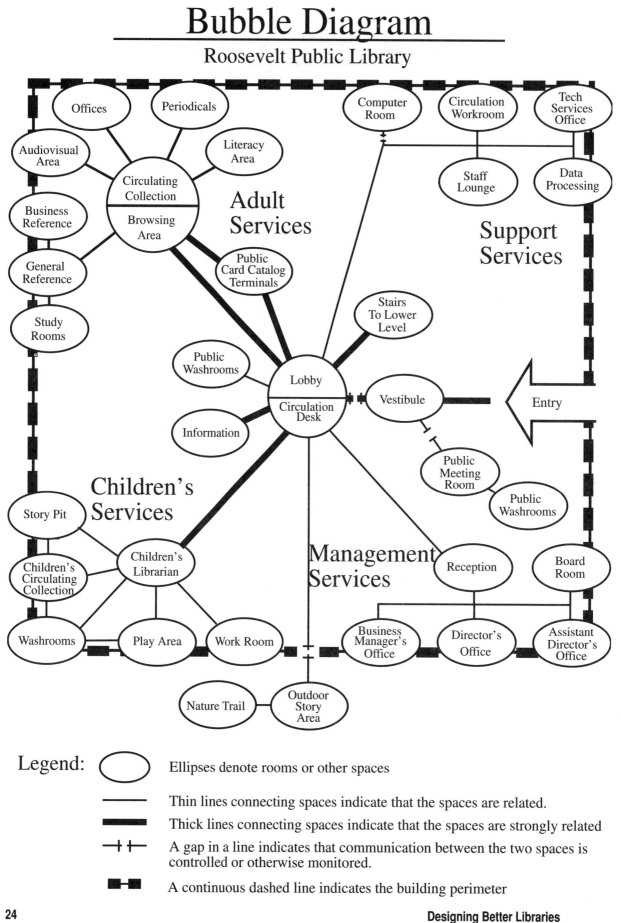

Legend:

⬭ Ellipses denote rooms or other spaces

—— Thin lines connecting spaces indicate that the spaces are related.

▬▬ Thick lines connecting spaces indicate that the spaces are strongly related

⊣⊢ A gap in a line indicates that communication between the two spaces is controlled or otherwise monitored.

▬ ▬ A continuous dashed line indicates the building perimeter been sculptured into face brick, often near the building entry. Decorative tile work, sometimes with hand-made tiles, can add interest to a wall or a floor. An impressive piece of custom woodwork for a circulation desk could be commissioned. If local artists and artisans can be utilized, including them in the project can be a good way to stimulate public interest and support for your project.

Site development: The building program should address the relationship between the building and the site. As a practical matter, creating adequate parking should always be considered. Access to and from the site should also be considered. There may be external restrictions that control where access points can be located. As an example, it is often difficult to gain permission from the municipal authorities to provide new curb cuts onto busy streets. Local zoning restrictions also have to be taken into account as they often limit the maximum amount of area that a building can occupy on a site, as well as mandate setback distances from the property lines and permissible building heights. While site design really begins later in the process with the schematic design, the client should express any desires or preconceptions relating to site development during the programming phase. Be sure to remember to include landscape design in your programming. All too often, landscape development is added as an afterthought or omitted entirely. When added as an afterthought, it is often the first thing cut if there is a budget crunch later on. We will take a closer look at the importance of landscaping when we discuss site analysis.

Other: Additional items that don't fit into any of the above categories will find their way into the "other" classification. Nearly anything could be included here: special safety or security requirements, information about unusual floor loadings (e.g., high structural loads from library stacks) or unusual acoustical requirements.

What the board and staff should do

Before programming can begin there are several things that the board and the staff should do.

Identify the project goals

The board should discuss the intended scope of the program statement with the architect before programming begins. Doing so will help insure that all the data that you think is important is going to be collected, this will also aid you in planning the amount of time that library staff will need to devote to the process.

In chapter two we spoke of "a house divided" and discussed the importance of having the support of the entire board and staff. Assuming that everyone is in favor of the project, this is the time to verify that there is agreement on the project goals. Examine your reasons for undertaking the project; these should be agreed upon in advance and will determine the conceptual "blueprint" for the project. Put your project goals in writing and refer to them from time to time to verify that the project is proceeding according to your plans.

Identify what you have

While identifying the project goals, spend some time identifying good and bad aspects of the facilities that you currently have. Identify things that work well for you and things that don't. Discuss the reasons for the shortcomings and successes and commit them to writing. For the architect these will be valuable clues that will help him or her tailor the programming to your project.

Discuss the programming goals with your architect

Request a list of goals for the programming process from your architect. They will vary from project to project but will usually include items like the following;

1. Identification of design questions.
2. Determination of potential project costs.
3. Development of project strategies that suit your circumstances.

Brainstorm

Get your staff together for some brainstorming sessions to try to identify their concerns and discuss their ideas. Include staff members that might not be scheduled for interviews with the architect to insure that they get their say in the programming process. Photocopy the architect's list of programming goals and the list of your project goals. Distribute the lists to staff members, this will give them an overview of what programming is about and will facilitate your brainstorming sessions.

Put together your project team

During the programming process the architect will be interviewing board and staff members to identify your needs. To control the process it is important to develop a list of responsibilities and assign them to members of your in-house team. It is critical that all the data generated in-house is reviewed before the architect is given the authority to act upon it. Questions that must be answered should include the following;

1. *Who will talk to the architects?* The board and the library director will probably be interviewed, but there are many others who should have input. Department heads should be on the list. Have them submit names of other staffers who they feel will contribute to the process. Staff members responsible for particular aspects of the library (like the computer system) should be included. The building engineer and others responsible for maintenance issues should be interviewed as much of the data collected has an impact on them.

2. *What is the "chain of command"?* Each person's contributions should be reviewed by his or her immediate superior to insure conformity to the overall goals of the project. This process should extend up to and including the board members with their ideas being reviewed by the board as a whole.

3. *Who will organize the effort?* Assign an individual at the library with the task of coordinating the interviews. Interviews and data collection can be time consuming. They must be scheduled and the staff involved must be allotted time for their participation. Determine a master schedule with your architect. Set a completion date and allot the time required to keep to your schedule.

Information gathering tools

The prime information gathering tool of the architect will be the interview. In addition to the interview, the architect may develop questionnaires and distribute them for the staff to complete. These questionnaires may address physical requirements for the building as well as staff and patron activities that occur within the library. The data from the questionnaires and from interviews will be evaluated and the often information is entered on "Room Data Sheets," which will summarize the requirements for each space. A sample room data sheet is shown on the next page to illustrate some of the questions that the architect may address.

Hard decisions

When the architect has completed the information-gathering portion of the programming phase, he or she will assemble the information into a preliminary program document that summarizes the data. This first compilation of the material represents the clients "wish list." At this point, the architect has the first indications of the size of the building and of the grade of the interior finishes. This can be used to arrive at a rough estimate of the project cost. There is usually a moment of truth the first time your dream is measured against your budget. There might not be a defined budget at this point, in which case the cost figures generated will be turned over to your financial consultant to determine the feasibility of the project. As often as not, expectations may exceed the available financial resources.

At this time the architect and the client have to sit down to make some hard decisions regarding the preliminary program. Square footages will have to be trimmed and some of the "bells and whistles" might have to be cut out entirely. The staff can be expected to do some internal lobbying for personal favorites. The final decisions as to what constitutes "bells and whistles" may have to be made by the library director and the board. Sometimes the cuts must go beyond the frills and will begin to erode important program elements. Your architect can help to show you the costs associated with different parts of the project and assist you in your decision making.

It is very important to bring the project within the anticipated budget before completing the program phase. Indeed, it is wise to establish a contingency of five to fifteen percent of the projected cost to make up for unanticipated cost overruns later. It can be tempting to proceed with the project when it is slightly over the proposed budget in the optimistic belief that the costs can be brought down by tightening up the design later. Unfortunately, it usually goes the other way. Inevitably, there are things that were forgotten or otherwise unaccounted for during programming, and they tend to get added to the building

Room Data Sheet

Programming / Schematic Design
Roosevelt Memorial Library

Date: July 27, 1994

Room Name: Library Director's Office Suite

Room Location: Administration Area

Furniture / Equipment	Mechanical / Electrical	Architectural
Furniture: One Desk Credenza 3 Chairs 1 File Cabinet Secretary/reception furniture similar but with typing return on desk and 3 additional file cabinets.	**Heating / Vent / AC:** Provide zoned heating and cooling for individual room control	**Floors:** Carpet
Equipment: Not Applicable	**Plumbing / Fixtures:** Not applicable	**Wall Partitions:** Drywall
Hours of Operation 10:00 a.m. to 4:00 p.m.	**Communications:** Networked Computer: Yes Telephone(s): Yes Other: Public address speaker in ceiling	**Ceilings:** Material: Lay-in acoustical Height: 8'-0"
Special Provisions:	**Electrical** Duplex outlets Recessed fluorescent fixtures with adequate illumination level for reading and writing.	**Doors / Windows:** Lockable, outward opening door with hold-open. No vision panel. Provide window with view to river.
Occupancy: Library Director	**Room Size:** Critical dimensions: Administrator's Office 12' x 15' Secretary/ receptionist 12' x 12' Total required Area: 324 sq. ft.	**Natural Lighting:** North window if possible

Additional Information:

Suite should be located in administration area and provide for easy access by staff and patrons.

Suite must be adjacent to business manager's office.

Provide coat closet.

Entry to office should be controlled by secretary/receptionist.

Provide wall space for 4'-0" wide x 5'-0" high framed photograph of library director.

BUSSARD, STEVER & TOTES - ARCHITECTS

later. Taken singly, they seem insignificant, but en masse they can put your project over budget.

A cautionary note...

The process of deleting items from your building program can be difficult. The building program produced thus far still represents the "wish list" of the people interviewed. It is a snapshot view of wishes and perceived needs of the library's users and staff at a particular point in time. It is thus imperative that flexibility be designed into the program to account for future needs. One must remember that in time, needs will change. It also must be noted that the current staff (including the board and the library director) will change with the passage of time. Sometimes, a building program can be unduly influenced by one or two people with strong personalities and set ideas. Remember that the building program you are developing now will have an impact on future generations of library staff, library directors, board members, and most importantly, patrons. In that light, all programming decisions should be measured against the perceived benefits for future users and administrators of the institution. It is not uncommon to find yourself having to navigate some difficult political waters at this time. Helping to bring resolution to difficult questions of priorities is one of the skills of a good architect. Let your architect guide the process and take the heat if need be. After all, leadership is one of the qualities that you are paying for.

The cost estimate

As the program begins to take shape, the architect will be able to start giving you information regarding the anticipated costs of the project. It is an easy matter to take the total of the square footages from the preliminary building program, multiply by an assumed cost per square foot and come up with a rough estimate of the project cost. The multiplication is simple; selecting the cost per square foot to use is not.

Many factors will affect the estimated cost per square foot. The size of the project, the geographic locale, the level of anticipated difficulty to construct the project and the relative expense of the interior finishes are a few of the factors that must be taken into account. These factors are always used along with general cost data from other local projects that are similar to your own. I had planned to include a table showing some sample costs per square foot for

different grades of construction. Consulting some of the various reference sources that I used in writing this book dissuaded me from that course. The effects of inflation can cause published numbers to be very misleading in these matters. One of the books was printed in 1977 and said that a library of "superb" quality could be built for $70 a square foot. Depending upon the circumstances, that number would now (almost 20 years later) be more than $150 a square foot. I caution the reader to take all published cost numbers with a grain of salt.

If you take a reasonable cost per square foot times the total of the areas itemized in your building program you will arrive at a number that, at first glance, seems to indicate the construction cost for your project. However, your analysis is lacking an important factor.

Building efficiency

The cost calculation above is based on the total of the program areas of the building. The square footage for each office, lobby, reading room, etc., is added up to produce a total program area. The term "program area" is significant. The building will be significantly larger than the program area. Just how much larger depends upon the building efficiency.

Building efficiency is defined as the net square footage (the areas described in your building program) divided by the gross area of the building. The gross area of the building includes not only the total of the areas from your building program, but the area occupied by mechanical spaces, corridors, wall thicknesses, storage areas, toilets, stairways, elevators, shafts, ducts and anything else not addressed in the program document. When including these other areas, your 40,000 square foot library may suddenly become a 66,000 square foot building, and your budget may suddenly look a lot more restrictive than it did a moment ago. In this example, the building efficiency would be expressed by the following:

Building Efficiency = Net Area÷Gross Area, thus;

Building Efficiency = 40,000 sq. ft. ÷ 66,000 sq. ft., which equals 0.61 or 61%.

You've got a number, 61%, but what does it mean? An opulent structure with wide hallways, expansive lobbies and sweeping stairways will have a relatively low efficiency ratio due to the percentage of the area taken up by those amenities. A warehouse with a large, open area and few hallways or other distractions will have a high efficiency. In a crude sense, the efficiency of your building is a reflection of the efficiency of your use of the public's money. The analogy is too limited to be of much use because few people would propose a warehouse for their public library, regardless of the efficiency of the building. On the other hand, the public probably would not support a grandiose structure for a small town library even if the municipal coffers would allow it. Building efficiencies typically range from 90% to 50%, depending on the building type. Describing efficiencies with appropriate adjectives is one of the best ways to visualize what the numbers mean. For a library, the following might be a rough guide.

Building Efficiency	Description
50%	Opulent, grand
60%	Monumental public building
65%	Comfortable
70%	Economical
75%	Austere
80%	Spartan
85% or higher	Probably impossible to attain for this type of use

The building efficiency has a direct bearing upon the public's perception of your library. The perception is equally colored by the selection of the interior finish materials. An expansive space with an "opulent" efficiency but cheap materials may strike you as stark rather than grand. A small, efficient building finished with interesting and high-quality materials might come off as comfortable and rich in detail.

Discuss and determine a target building efficiency with your architect. You need only address the issue in the most general of terms. As long as the board of directors understands the balance between building efficiency, economy and public perception they will be able to arrive at informed decisions regarding their building. When looking at an architect's space analysis of your project, you should be able to find a figure for the efficiency that he or she is assuming, and thus verify that you and the architect have similar ideas of what kind of building you are developing.

The final product

After you have completed the difficult stage of reducing your square footage to fall within your budget and agreed upon a target building efficiency, your architect can produce the final program document. This combination of written and graphic material will provide the foundation upon which the rest of the architectural project is built. The document will include many of the items that have been discussed here as well as additional information that is applicable to your project. At this point you will have the information to evaluate the building or addition, and a good idea of its potential cost.

Sign-off

You should now schedule a board meeting so the board of trustees as well as management staff can sign-off on the project to date. All people involved should be given a copy of the document a week or so in advance to allow everybody to have a chance to thoroughly review the material. Ideally, major changes suggested in previous reviews have been incorporated into the document. If any other changes seem required, make a written list of them, attach them to a copy of the program and give an additional copy of the changes to the architect. Have the board members and management staff sign the master program document to indicate their acceptance of it. This master copy of the program with attached changes should be retained for reference. Any changes to the program after acceptance could provide a legitimate basis for the architect to bill you for the additional time involved in rewriting parts of the program.

Onward!

Your project is now off and running. You have a good idea of what you are going to do, and now it remains to determine how and where you are going to do it. We shall next look at another phase of the architectural process that is often considered to be an additional service—Site Analysis.

Notes

1. American Institute of Architects. Document B141. Standard Form of Agreement Between Owner and Architect. Washington, DC: The Institute, 1987.

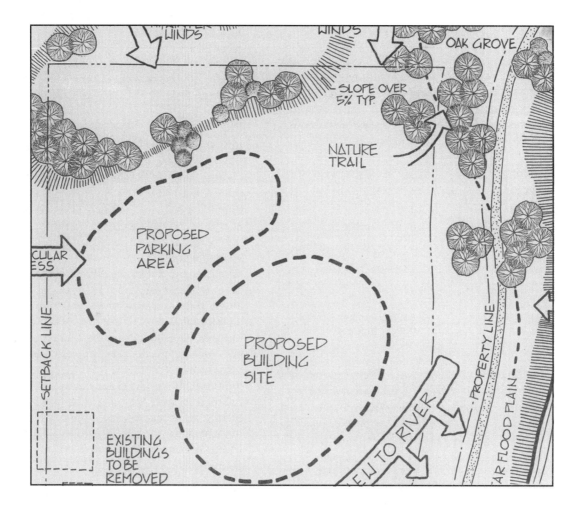

6

Site Analysis

Location, Location, Location!
Realtor's maxim

This is the place! **Brigham Young**

I'll never forget a story that was related to me by an acquaintance. He was the structural engineer for an office building in Chicago. The building site had been selected and purchased by the owner. The location was perfect, and tenants were already lining up to sign leases. Small structures on the site had been razed, and several borings had been taken to test the strength of the underlying soil and rock. All appeared well. Construction schedules were established, manpower mobilized and building permits obtained. The schedule was tight, but with good weather the building could be finished on time. A construction fence was erected around the construction site. The fence was solid wood with the obligatory peepholes cut into it so children and other interested passersby could keep track of the work. Early one weekend morning, large, costly excavating equipment was brought in. Everything was ready.

Just after dawn on Monday morning the excavators arrived. Equipment was checked, and the air filled with blue diesel smoke as cold engines were started. The time clocks started ticking as the hourly rates for the large machinery kicked in and across town, the first dump trucks were

on their way to pick up the excavated material. The work began well, and a steady stream of trucks rumbled back and forth past glass-fronted office buildings.

He got the phone call at around ten that morning.

Arriving at the construction site he saw a group of workers standing around the excavation, looking in the hole. The diesel engines had been shut down, and there was a line of dump trucks waiting to be filled. Nothing was moving. It's not unusual to find pieces of old foundations while excavating in an urban setting. However, this was much more than a piece. Partially exposed at the bottom of the hole was a mass of concrete. There, neatly sandwiched between the locations of their soil borings, was a foundation for a turn-of-the-century railroad roundhouse. The foundation was many feet thick and liberally reinforced with what appeared to be railroad rails. Blasting is discouraged in most downtown areas, so the only thing to do was to jack-hammer it into small pieces and truck it away, a time-consuming and expensive proposition.

The construction schedule was shot, and the cost of the additional work would have to be borne by the owner. The excavators drove off, the dump trucks left, even the sidewalk superintendents at the peepholes went home. The engineer was left with the unenviable task of having to call the owner with the news.

The frustrated building owner in the story might also have thought "This is the place!" when he first saw the site. It was just that there was a lot more to the place than he realized. There's no guarantee that a site analysis will protect you from surprises like the one that he got, but it will at least help tip the scales in your favor.

In the last chapter, we touched on the importance of the relationship between a building and its site. For a building project, site analysis is the first step in the design process. Like programming, much of site analysis involves the collection and interpretation of data. Some of the information is readily accessible. Some of the information requires detective work, intuition and the assistance of specialized consultants to uncover.

A site analysis includes much more than a search for forgotten foundations. In a moment we will discuss the scope of a complete site analysis and what the board should be doing during this phase; but first, let's talk about the role of another design professional, the landscape architect.

The landscape architect

For the sake of simplicity I'm using the word "architect" to describe the person who is providing your site analysis. Many times the analysis is provided by an architect, but often, much of the work might be done by a landscape architect. Like an architect, the landscape architect is trained in design. However, their focus is on site development and plant materials. Although architects often produce site designs, the special skills and expertise of the landscape architect can make this individual especially suited for inclusion in the site analysis. If you are not contemplating any building projects and are just looking for ways to spruce up the look of your building, consider retaining a landscape architect to suggest some ways to make better use of your site. First impressions do count, and the first impression of a building will often be made by the landscaping rather than the structure itself.

What the board should do

Even a building addition will require a site analysis, but for the moment, let's assume that you are purchasing a new site for your project. You've probably looked around town for appropriate sites and maybe even set a realtor on the scent. Say that two potential sites seem to stand out from the others, and now it only remains to decide between those two.

In a case like this, it may be advisable to have your architect do a partial analysis for each site and apply a numerical ranking to the different aspects studied. With this method the choice between the sites might be made easier if there is a clear winner when the scores are added up. If there's no clear winner, you at least have a lot more information that you can factor into your decision making. You can discuss the thoroughness of each partial site analysis with your architect and decide on the minimum number of aspects that might be investigated in order to provide enough data to allow you to make an informed decision. In this case, you reserve the complete site analysis for the selected site and thus reduce your expenses for professional services.

While narrowing down the number of sites, the board should discuss the project and how they imagine the building would relate to each site. A number of factors enter into the selection of a building site: emotional reactions to different parts of town, political factors, historical significance, the cost of the site and the ease of access—to name a few. These subjects alone can provide the basis for a lot of discussion, and other aspects will no doubt surface.

What you should provide

Before beginning a thorough site analysis, some preliminary information will usually have to be supplied to the architect. The client customarily pays for and obtains soil borings and a survey of the property. The architect will require this information as early as possible to do a site analysis. If the library hasn't yet purchased the property, the current owner may be able to provide a survey and might even be persuaded to pay for the cost of the soil borings. The locations and number of the soil borings are usually suggested by the architect based on the potential placement of the building and other site improvements. Ask your architect if there are any other pieces of information that he or she will require up front. An environmental assessment of the site may also be required, your architect and local building authorities will be able put you in contact with an appropriate consultant if you wish.

Get a survey

If you are building an addition to your existing facility, or own the property on which you propose to build, this is the time to order a survey of your building and/or property. Your architect can assist you in retaining a surveyor if you do not already have a relationship with one. If you already have an up-to-date survey, a new one may not be required; again, your architect can help you determine if any existing surveys are suitable.

What the architect should do

A complete site analysis will cover aspects ranging from the aesthetic to the technical. As is often the case, the architect will be assembling a team of other professionals representing various fields. The team might include landscape architects, civil engineers, land planners, soils engineers, environmental engineers and others.

Site analysis is not included as a part of the "basic services" in the standard owner/architect agreement. Many architects will include it as a part of the overall design process. Ask your architect if he or she plans to provide it as a part of the package. If your situation requires that the architect analyze several sites, you will probably have to pay for additional professional services. When negotiating a contract with the architect make sure that everyone has the same understanding of which services are going to be provided as a part of the basic package and which ones will incur additional fees.

The first step in the site analysis is a careful examination of the building program. The program can determine, to a large extent, how a site will be utilized. The architect must then determine whether or not a program and a site are compatible. Each must be evaluated with respect to the other. If preliminary work establishes that the program and site are suited for one another, the process of site analysis and site design can begin.

Probably the first thing that the architect will do is to verify that the building and other planned improvements will fit on the site. Many other site deficiencies can be remedied given enough money, but if it's too small, the rest of the site analysis is rendered a moot point. It's not usually a problem to get the building itself on the site, the problem often lies in accommodating the parking lot. The percentage of modern sites that are covered by parking lots is shocking. For many projects parking lots occupy over twice the area covered by the building. The exact number of parking spaces required will often be set by local zoning ordinances. Change seems unlikely as long as the family car remains the primary mode of transportation; unless that fact is altered they will continue (in the words of Joni Mitchell) to "pave paradise and put up a parking lot."

The following is a checklist of some items that should be considered on a site analysis. Discuss the list with your architect to verify the depth of the analysis that he or she is proposing to provide. If something that you think is important is left out, ask that it be included. If you are buying a building site and haven't retained an architect yet, this list may be used as a guide to aid you with your site selection.

✔ Existing Conditions

Size: As mentioned above, the size of the site is one of the most basic considerations. The true buildable area of the site may be much smaller than is apparent. Many of the factors listed below will have an impact on the buildable area of the site.

Flood plains: If some of the building site lies under a flood plain, that portion is usually unusable for construction. Parking lots may often be constructed on a flood plain. The architect will research the site to determine the existence and extent of flood plains.

Wetlands: If your site has any designated wetlands on it, you will usually be prohibited from building on those areas. In certain circumstances, a building can be put in a wetlands area if another area of the site is "transformed" into a wetland. This transformation from regular land to wetland is somewhat controversial and may eventually be disallowed by the federal government. A word of warning—you cannot always determine what is and what isn't a "wetlands" area by a casual inspection of the site. Standing water is only one clue that the site may contain wetlands. The types of plants growing on the site, as well as soil types are also taken into consideration. To the lay person it may in fact seem somewhat arbitrary whether or not a site is designated as a wetland. Be that as is may, the site must be evaluated for wetlands before any building plans are considered.

Endangered species: The existence and potential effect of the project upon endangered species will also be evaluated. This evaluation as well as the wetlands study will usually be performed by an environmental engineer retained by the architect.

Availability of utilities: For most urban sites, utilities will be available for your use. However, in rural and suburban settings the type and capacity of the utilities around your site can impose serious limitations on your project. The team put together by your architect will make a thorough investigation of these utilities and incorporate the data that they collect into their site analysis.

The utilities that they study will include: electrical supplies, natural gas, water, telephone, sanitary sewer and storm sewer. The sewer systems will be investigated by the architect's civil engineer. Natural gas and electrical services will be researched by the architect's mechanical and electrical engineers respectively. Site analysis, like much of architecture, is a group effort. Your architect is responsible for insuring that all the varied players are working in concert and in accordance with the building program.

Utility easements: Your seemingly wide open site may have a natural gas pipeline, water main or buried electrical lines running through it or along one of the property lines. An easement of a defined width will prohibit any construction over or near the utility. The site survey should identify such easements

Subsurface investigations: Soil borings will provide information on the ability of the soil to support a building. They will also identify the level of the ground water table, which may have a dramatic effect on the cost of constructing a basement.

Topography: The topography of the site will be analyzed to determine its impact on the proposed development. A hilly site can be more aesthetically pleasing than a flat one, but the costs of earth moving for the building and parking lots goes up. The difficulty of making the site accessible to the handicapped is also increased.

☑ History of the Site

Former uses: Research into the former uses of a site is invaluable. There's a nearly infinite number of items (including foundations from railroad roundhouses) that might lie just below the surface. Subsurface surprises are almost never welcome ones. The architect may spend time studying old surveys, atlases and city directories, attempting to identify what was there. For rural sites there is usually little information to go on, and few problems are typically encountered. For urban sites the research may be in-depth and the risks are higher.

Buried tanks and hazardous materials: Finding that there was formerly a gas station or oil company on your site is often an indication of troubles ahead. Federal environmental legislation mandates that you remove buried tanks and clean up chemical contamination. There are other, less obvious hazards, like solvents and heavy metal contamination from old factories. There was a good example of this in my home town, Elgin, Illinois. A project that was being built on the former site of the Elgin National Watch Company suffered long delays because it was discovered that watch dials and radium had been dumped on the site when the factory was in operation. Construction was halted until the material could be removed; not an inexpensive project.

Landfills: It's amazing how often old landfills turn up. Most of them were not the municipal operations that are now the norm. Landfilling was, until recently, the accepted way to both get rid of your garbage and raise the grade of part of your property to make it more usable. Foundations cannot be placed on filled material, thus the material must be removed before a building can be built. Soil borings will indicate the presence of old landfills.

Archeological considerations: In many states an archeological inventory of the site is mandatory. Finding that there is a Native American burial ground or the remains of a frontier settlement on your property is intellectually interesting, but it often means long delays before construction can begin while the artifacts are studied. Contractors know this, and there are many stories of excavation work speeding up dramatically in an effort to remove old bones or pottery shards before anyone else spots them. The archeological inventory is often provided by the state, and thus must often be scheduled well in advance of construction.

✔ Municipal Restrictions

Allowable uses: Local zoning ordinances will usually define the allowable uses for a site.

Setbacks: Local zoning restrictions will often stipulate how far a building must be set back from the property lines. These setbacks can prohibit construction on a significant percentage of the site.

Allowable building area: Zoning restrictions can also determine the maximum percentage of a site that can be covered by a building.

Historical districts: If your site is located in a designated historic district there may be regulations which limit your building design to particular architectural styles. A study of any applicable historic district restrictions as well as the other municipal restrictions will be a part of a zoning analysis. Your architect will nearly always perform a zoning analysis for your project.

✔ Site Accessibility and Circulation

Access to the site: Easy site access is an integral part of serving the public. Access should be available to both vehicles and pedestrians. Traffic flow to your site is out of your control but you can control circulation within your site. In chapter five we mentioned the potential problems in obtaining curb cuts on busy thoroughfares. There are other considerations that must be negotiated with state and local authorities. If your library is on a heavily traveled street, you may wish to investigate whether or not it is possible to get turning lanes at your entry points. Another consideration might be a traffic light. The architect can coordinate these negotiations for you.

As you will potentially be dealing with city, township, county or state governmental agencies there can be a long lead time in obtaining curb cuts, turning lanes and traffic lights. I have assumed, of course, that the authorities have agreed to your requests. Sometimes they won't. If the site you'd like to purchase absolutely requires an entry drive off Augusta Avenue in order to make the internal circulation work properly, have your architect obtain written approval for the drive from the appropriate authorities before you buy.

If your site isn't on a busy street, you may run into a different set of problems. It's possible to overtax the traffic capacity of the surrounding streets, usually to the dismay of the neighbors. You are left with trying to maintain a delicate balance, the access streets must neither be too big nor too small. In real life, the access streets are seldom ideal. With good planning and some negotiation, your architect will help you to squeeze the most from your site.

Internal circulation: The potential points of entry for your building site will dictate much of the circulation within your site. Safety and convenience, in that order, are the primary goals for internal circulation. Libraries generate quite a bit of traffic from all age groups. New parents pushing strollers, high-schoolers squealing the tires on their parents' cars, and retirees are all competing for space in the parking lot. Whenever there is a mixture of automobiles and pedestrians, extra care is required to insure a safe site.

Other important considerations regarding internal site circulation include pedestrian routes from the parking lot to the building, access for emergency vehicles and the accessibility of the site for the handicapped. Since the passage of the Americans With Disabilities Act (ADA), there are for the first time, uniform federal design standards to insure that all public sites are made accessible. All public buildings must conform to the standards set forth in the ADA.

Barriers: For building sites in hilly areas accessibility can become a challenging issue. For example, say that your building is built on a hillside with the building on the uphill side and the parking lot on the lower portion, five feet below the elevation of your main entry. Five foot difference in elevation, or 60", doesn't seem like a terribly long climb. At the standard seven inches maximum rise per stair that's only nine steps. However, to accommodate a wheelchair 60" difference in elevation means 70' of wheelchair ramp including two landings and possibly switchbacks in addition. Not only is the difference in elevation difficult for the wheelchair user to negotiate, but it can be difficult for the architect and landscape architect to integrate the ramp into the site design.

✔ Climate

Orientation: The "orientation" of a building refers to its placement with respect to the path of the sun and the prevailing winds. In temperate climates, the rule of thumb is to place most of the windows facing south and to keep the north side free from too many openings that will allow the north winds to rob your building of heat in the winter. To prevent direct sunlight from entering in the summer and increasing your cooling bills, wide overhangs can be placed over south-facing windows to provide shade from the high summer sun and admit only the lower, winter sun.

Each site also has special conditions that will effect the desired placement and orientation of your building. Tall buildings on a neighboring property, a nearby grove of pine trees or an adjacent lake must all be considered. Any of these features can modify what is known as the "microclimate" of your site. Program requirements must also be taken into account. A library with a large rare book collection for example, might be better designed with few windows to minimize fading of the collection due to the ultraviolet component of sunlight. A busy street might also be a reason to limit the number of openings on that face of the building to keep down the noise level inside.

For every limitation, a building site will offer an opportunity. Proper orientation of the building will insure that your get the maximum benefit from your site. Visit the building site with your architect and landscape architect to discuss its qualities. Let them know what you think is important, what you want to see and hear and what distractions you want to avoid.

✔ Landscaping

The landscape plan: While the complete site design will be developed later on, a complete site analysis will usually include at least a preliminary landscape plan. We discussed some of the advantages of landscaping in chapter three. Landscaping will address both aesthetic and practical considerations. Ground-covers will soften hard edges and define walkways. Well-placed trees will provide shade, guide circulation and enhance your building at the same time. Flowers will add beauty and can direct attention to selected site elements like signs or entries.

The landscape architect also uses many non-plant materials to achieve desired effects. Railroad ties might retain soil in a planting area, bark chips could define a path to an outdoor area for children's programs. Re-creations of antique lamp posts might be used to provide exterior lighting if your library is in an historic neighborhood. Local stone might provide an interesting material for walls and planters.

A good landscape plan will add a softer, more human touch to your building. While it may seem expensive at the time, an investment of a few tens-of-thousands of dollars spent on trees and other landscape materials will pay back impressive dividends as the plants mature. The importance of exterior terraces, walks and screens should also be considered. An added advantage to landscaping is that it can often increase the energy efficiency of your building. During summer months in temperate climates deciduous trees can provide shade and effectively reduce your cooling costs. In winter months the leaves have fallen and sunshine will warm and brighten the interior spaces. Coniferous trees on the north and west sides will protect both against winter winds and late afternoon summer sun which can otherwise increase air conditioning costs.

In northeastern Illinois where I live, suburbs are expanding around Chicago and new housing developments dot the prairie. These places all seem to have one thing in common: last week they were cornfields. After driving through interchangeable subdivisions with their endless chemically greened lawns, I am always relieved to get back to my 1920's era neighborhood where mature maple trees line the streets and the results of 70 years worth of weekend yard projects blend into a rich and varied mixture. Remember that your building is going to be there for a long time, easily long enough for an ambitious landscape plan to mature.

There, there

Speaking of Oakland, California, Gertrude Stein said "There is no there there." I feel much the same in those anonymous suburbs. Landscaping is one of the things that can transform a building site into a place. Whether your library is modest or grand, it deserves a place.

✔ Outdoor Activities

Outdoor spaces: A building site offers a lot more than a place to set a building and a parking lot. A hillside might be sculpted to provide a seating area for children during a story telling or musical program, a nature walk could be designed and plants selected to illustrate the changing of the seasons to grade schoolers. Butterfly gardens, with flowers and plants specially selected to appeal to different species of butterflies and moths can be planted where they will be visible from reading areas. You and your architect can explore such opportunities during the site design.

What the architect should give you

At the end of the site analysis phase of a project your architect should present the results of the analysis to the board and the management staff. Much of the site analysis will be presented in graphic form. The architect, armed with display boards and pointer, may appear before the board to make the presentation and to answer questions.

The presentation boards should illustrate the site with an assumed building footprint superimposed upon it. I say "assumed" because at this early stage of the design, the shape of the building has not been completely defined. Traffic flow and parking should be indicated as should surrounding streets. Topography is often shown along with the site drainage patterns.

Building setbacks, easements and rights-of-way may be shown on the presentation boards, these graphic interpretations of the site limitations are a great aid to understanding the possibilities of your site. Significant vegetation and other landscape features should also be illustrated as they will have a great impact on the placement and orientation of your building.

Specialized site plans may also be presented, some may only show soil types to illustrate which portions of the site are buildable, other plans may illustrate the extent of wetlands or flood plains. Opportunities for views and adjacent land uses also might be shown. Of course, the number of plans presented and the extent of the information that they cover will depend entirely upon your own circumstances. A building addition will need only a minimum amount of site analysis, while a cluster of new buildings on a large site might require a master plan as well as smaller-scale site analyses. The graphic material provided by the architect can also be used as presentation materials for public inspection as a part of a referendum campaign.

Some written information might also be presented. Soil reports, surveys and a verbal summary of the site analysis are often bound into a report. The large presentation boards can be reduced and included in the report to provide a complete site analysis document at a manageable size. The scope of your site analysis and the extent of the materials that the architect prepares should be set out in advance and incorporated into the owner/architect contract at the beginning of the project. We will get into those considerations later, when we discuss selecting and hiring architects.

Sign-off

In previous chapters I indicated that I recommend a formal sign-off at the end of each phase of the project. Have the architect include a formal sign-off sheet at the end of the program analysis documents. The board members and the library director should sign this page to indicate their formal acceptance of the site analysis and to indicate their approval of the completed work and the direction of the project. Their signatures indicate the close of the site analysis phase and confirm that any additional site analysis work they request of the architect might result in a need for additional compensation. If the architect has not produced all of the items that were previously agreed upon, the board should discuss the matter with the architect. It may turn out that some of the services agreed to were not applicable to the site in question. Usually, a brief discussion can resolve these questions to the satisfaction of the board and either the board will sign the document, or the architect will be directed to produce the remaining items before the sign-off will be completed.

With the close of the site analysis and the building program in hand, the architect and the board are ready to begin the building design. If all the players have been active in the programming and site analysis, they will have developed a working relationship that should enable them to successfully navigate their way through the design process.

7
Building Design

...it shall be framed upon a single, noble motive, to which the design of all its parts, in some more or less subtle way, shall be confluent and helpful. **Frederick Olmstead**

The physician can bury his mistakes, but the architect can only advise his clients to plant vines. **Frank Lloyd Wright**

If you ask the average person what an architect does, the answer will often be something to the effect of "design buildings." Although architects spend much of their time performing other tasks, design remains the heart of the profession. Design has an impact on us all, almost anyone could probably name an example of a building that they find particularly pleasing, bad or inappropriate.

Many forms of art are experienced in a fleeting fashion, during a walk past a sculpture on a downtown plaza or perhaps on an annual visit to an art museum. However, a building is a work of art in which you live and work. Granted, it's not necessarily a significant artwork, but countless design decisions are made in planning even the simplest and most utilitarian of buildings. There are exceptions to every rule; it's difficult to find the spark of creativity in the prefabricated metal buildings that are now replacing old barns across America, and some utilitarian structures like telephone switching stations are virtually nothing more than brick clad boxes. That doesn't have to be the case.

Of buildings and boxes

I recently read of the impending demolition of an old electrical substation near where I live. It wasn't significant in a design sense, but it was a pleasing building. Arched windows, nice brickwork and considered proportions lent it a grace lacking in many of the later buildings that surrounded it. You could tell that this building, as simple as it was, was designed. Somebody had thought about it. In contrast, some of its more recent cousins appear to have been installed rather than designed. For a period of time culminating in the 1960s, there was movement toward eliminating what was perceived to be "unnecessary" and "applied" detail on buildings. In the hands of a master architect like Mies van der Rohe, this style found form in some powerful and elegant buildings that are landmarks in recent architectural history. In the hands of others, it resulted in swarms of buildings that were little more than boxes; some were glass, some were brick, some were metal, some were stone, some were combinations of materials, but they were still boxes.

The look was so sought after that many turn of the century buildings on small town main streets were "modernized" by covering them with painted metal panels to make them appear to be closer to the ideal of the box. Perhaps the goal was to have entire cities that looked installed rather than designed. The results never looked as "clean" as their makers intended; they were invariably cluttered with things like street numbers which were becoming more necessary than ever in order to tell the buildings apart.

We seem to have at least temporarily outgrown the need to cover up what is old; indeed, an older building is now often perceived as a status symbol. Rehabbing old warehouses and industrial buildings for upscale clients is the current vogue, although the results aren't necessarily any more imaginative or successful than were the boxes of a few decades ago.

Compromise, creativity and Gary Cooper

In doing research for this book, I read everything that I could lay my hands on concerning the practice of architecture and the nature of the architect/client relationship. I even went to our local library and checked out a video tape of *The Fountainhead*, the 1949 film version of Ayn Rand's book in which Gary Cooper plays Howard Roark, an idealistic architect fighting a personal battle to avoid compromising his principals in order to merely please the crowd.

I jumped at the chance to see him play the role of the heroic, misunderstood yet brilliant architect. I could really identify with this character. Please forgive me if I summarize the plot for those who haven't read the book or seen the film.

In the film, Howard Roark suffers a number of career setbacks. To make ends meet he is forced to allow another architect to use one of his designs for a building. The other architect yields to business pressures and allows the design to be changed to make it more in keeping with the client's idea of what the public really wants. Howard is so upset by this that he goes to the site and dynamites the partially completed building. The client is understandably upset by this turn of events and insists on legal action. After an impassioned courtroom speech in which Howard takes the jury from the discovery of fire to the advent of totalitarianism, (remember this is 1949) a "not guilty" verdict is returned. The rights of the individual are upheld and the prerogative of the designer is protected. Somehow, the client's right to get

what he was paying for was left out of the equation. The movie guide book on my bookshelf generously awards *The Fountainhead* two and a half stars.

In actual practice, architects seldom blow up buildings that they don't like. I conducted an impromptu poll and couldn't find any of my peers who would admit to doing so.

The working relationship

Howard Roark would attest to the fact that design is the most emotionally charged part of a project. While designing, the architect must seek the balance between his or her creative impulse and the practical needs of the client. Architecture is art that solves problems. To a degree, compromise is always part of the process. Buildings must conform to the site. Budgetary realities have to be recognized, and the wishes of the client must be taken into consideration. A successful design addresses those limitations and transcends them. Your role in the design process is to work with your architect and to do what you can to help to foster the working relationship that exists between you.

The quality of the relationship between the client and the architect will have a great impact on the design process. Some clients want a lot of involvement and may wish to have a say in all but the most minor of design decisions. Others may want only a broad oversight of the architect's work and may be content to see the design only at certain milestone points. Sometimes the project is handed to the architect who then has carte blanche to solve the problems as he or she sees fit, as long as the final result conforms to the budget and the program requirements. Most projects are of the second type; the design proceeds and is reviewed by the client at certain, predetermined times. This is probably the most efficient method. It frees the architect and the client from constant meetings dealing with project minutia, yet provides enough oversight to reduce the chances of a major redrawing of the plans when the design is finally presented.

The design phase is typically broken up into two distinct parts—schematic design and design development. Each part has its own roles for the architect and for the client. A good understanding of the design process will enable you to get the greatest benefit from your architect and will help insure to that you will get the product you want.

SCHEMATIC DESIGN

Schematic design can be a little difficult to separate from design development as the separation of the two phases is a little arbitrary. Design is a process that continues throughout the project, from programming through construction. Separating design into two parts is convenient in terms of the architect's billing for professional services and helps to insure adequate client involvement during the design phase by offering a predetermined milestone point for review of the design. Under the AIA Standard Form of Agreement Between Owner and Architect, schematic design represents 15 percent of the architect's fee.

What the architect does

In schematic design the architect begins with the building program and the site analysis that were produced during the pre-design phase and approved by the owner. Schematic design represents the first effort to determine the relative sizes and interrelationships of the elements that were defined in the building program. The prime objective is to arrive at a clearly defined, feasible concept and to present it in a form that is understandable to the client. The secondary objectives are to clarify the building program, explore the most promising alternative design solutions, and to develop a reliable basis for analyzing the estimated cost of the project.

What's the big idea?

Many aspects of the design and of the general philosophy will be discussed with the client during the schematic design phase. This is the time when many of the major decisions regarding the basic plan and look of your building will be made. The overall concept behind the building design, sometimes called the "big idea" is generated and reviewed with the owner. The "big idea" may take the form of a very simple and somewhat abstract phrase like "a circle within a square," or it can take the form of a quick, conceptual sketch based upon a single, strong form like a major axis with branches radiating off of it. Whatever form it takes, the concept is an ordering mechanism for the architect and offers a point of beginning. It is

intended to narrow the range of solutions being explored and gives the project direction.

Rough designs will begin to be developed. At this point, they may still take the form of bubble diagrams, but the relative sizes of the bubbles will be adjusted to begin to correspond to the relative sizes of the spaces that they represent. At this stage, many alternative solutions may be drawn. As the solutions are refined and reviewed with the owner, many of them will be dropped and the field will be limited to just a few of the most promising ones.

The project schedule will be refined at this time. Though long-term schedules can be difficult to keep, they are very important in monitoring the progress of the work. The architect should keep the board appraised of any changes to the schedule as the project commences.

At the close of schematic design the architect will usually make a formal presentation to the board. There should be few surprises if everybody has been involved in the process. The formal presentation will often be made at a board meeting, thus giving the public and the media their first opportunity to see what's in store for the library.

What the board should do

The board should take an active role in the schematic design process to insure that the project is evolving according to their wishes. At the start of the schematic design phase a number of meetings should be scheduled with the architect. These meetings need not be formal presentations, but at the very least the architect should show the board what design options are being considered and be able to state the rationale behind each of them.

Take the time to study each of the proposed solutions and be prepared to voice any concerns during the review meetings. It is best that your comments be delivered to the architect before the entire board so each may know where the others stand. It is vitally important to build a board consensus during schematic design as subsequent changes can be expensive and might effect the project schedule.

Cost estimates should be scrutinized, shared with financial consultants and the library's legal counsel and compared against the available funds. During schematic design it sometimes it becomes apparent that the project cannot be built with the available funding. In this case additional funding will have to be sought or the building program trimmed to bring it within budget. This harkens back to the "hard decisions" we discussed in chapter five. If the program must be significantly cut, extra meetings should be called with the project team and the architect to reach a resolution.

Cut 'em some slack

Leave the architect some room to do his or her job. Sometimes clients approach an architect to do a project with set, preconceived ideas. It's sometimes expressed as "We know exactly what we want, and all you have to do is draw it." This is a good news-bad news proposition for the architect. The good news is that the clients have probably already given a lot of thought to their project and may have a clear idea of their needs. The bad news is that some of their ideas might be inappropriate when taken in the larger context of the program, the site analysis, building codes, affordability, etc. Let the architect know your concepts for the building but try to maintain an open mind if the schematic designs the architect produces don't exactly fit your ideas. Remember that you are paying this person for his or her expertise. To get the most for your money, don't maintain too tight a rein.

Have your building engineer review the architect's recommendations for mechanical, electrical and plumbing systems to verify that the types of equipment that the architect is proposing are within the capabilities of your staff to operate and maintain. As the demand for energy efficiency increases, so does the complexity of the systems that are going into today's buildings. Sometimes training seminars will be offered by the companies that manufacture the equipment. If the new systems are significantly more complicated than the old, ask your engineer to explore the avenues for additional training.

Ask the architect to provide a proposed schedule for the design and construction of the building. Evaluate the schedule in light of your needs. Architects have every incentive to try to get their portion of the work completed as soon as possible; in most cases the longer that jobs drag on, the less they make per hour of effort. If the estimate for the project construction time exceeds your timetable, discuss ways to speed

up the process with your architect. There are alternatives like fast-track construction which, for a price, can speed up the process.

An eye towards the future

There is one aspect of building design that you could insist on—making accommodations for future expansion. Ask the architect to provide an avenue for expanding your building should it ever become necessary. Having the flexibility to be able to add on to your building (and parking) at a future date could well save some future building committee from having to decide to relocate in order to accommodate expanding library needs. Even if you do wind up relocating, having the potential for expansion will often mean that your building will command a higher selling price. It's usually a good move to leave yourself some options.

Changes

If the board requests significant changes to the schematic design at one of the review points, make sure that the request is given to the architect in written form; meeting minutes will suffice. This is done to help reduce the chances of any misunderstandings regarding the board's wishes and to have a written record of the course of the project.

It is very important that your internal chain of command be defined and in place. The architect should have a set way of receiving instructions regarding changes to the work. I've seen many cases where an architect made revisions to a project only to discover later that the person asking for the changes had no real authority to do so. The end result can be a partial re-draw, bad feelings within the project team and possibly a request for additional fees on the part of the architect. For the outsider, it is not always obvious who has the authority in your organization. Sit down with the architect at the beginning of the project and work out how instructions are to be transmitted. In the case of a public library they might be required to be in writing and bear the signatures of the library director and the president of the board.

Finally, the end of schematic design represents another milestone point in your project. The board should again sign off on each item presented to indicate their acceptance of the work done to date.

What the architect should give you

After the schematic design phase of a project is completed, the owner can typically expect to have one or more conceptual building designs in-hand. At this stage of the project, these design solutions may even be freehand drawings. They are not intended to show the exact sizes and placement of all the parts of the building, but rather express the building program information in a graphic manner.

Price estimates are also typically generated at this time. As the building begins to take shape, the accuracy of the estimated prices begins to increase. Many architects use professional price estimators. If you are using a small to medium-sized architectural firm, chances are that it does not have a professional estimator on staff. I advise the board to encourage the architect to retain an independent estimator to give detailed cost estimates at several points during the project. This could even be stipulated in the owner/architect agreement. The cost will, of course, be eventually footed by the library as the architect will build it into the fee, but it is a good and relatively inexpensive insurance that can help to identify potential problems while there is still time to make changes.

The following is a checklist of items that are often included in a schematic design.

☑ Small scale floor plans

Floor plans will be included in the schematic design presentation. Depending on the project, they may be little more than bubble diagrams drawn to scale, or they might be recognizable floor plans at a small scale—usually at $^1/16$ inch equals one foot. This small scale keeps the level of detail to a minimum and reflects the degree of refinement of the design at this point.

☑ Building elevations

Building elevations (straight-on views of each face of the building) should be included. Note that elevations can be misleading. Since they are drawn without perspective, parts of the building that are more distant from the viewing position are not drawn smaller than other parts of the building that are close up. Because of this, elevations can be difficult to interpret.

☑ Building sections

One or two building sections should be included, these may be at the same small scale as the floor plans. A building section depicts an imaginary slice made vertically through the building and illustrates the relationship of foundations, floors, ceilings, mechanical spaces and roofs.

☑ Site plan

A schematic site plan should show the building placement, parking lots, anticipated site circulation and major landscape features. As with the building floor plans, the plan may be drawn at a small scale.

☑ Outline specification

The specification is a written document which sets the standards of quality for the construction, names products and materials which will be accepted, and itemizes additional responsibilities of the contractor. An outline specification is a very general description of the work; it will give a broad overview of building systems and materials.

☑ Preliminary estimates of construction cost

The estimated construction cost should be furnished. Large contingencies are typically included to cover for unanticipated conditions. The contingencies can be reduced somewhat as the design is developed.

☑ Documentation of mechanical, electrical and plumbing systems

During schematic design the architect will begin to coordinate the work of the various other professionals who will contribute to the project. The schematic design should have, at a minimum, written descriptions of the mechanical and electrical systems that are being considered for the building. The preliminary design of these systems is an important part of early planning and is required for accurate, early estimates of the construction cost.

✔ Renderings

Detailed renderings are not included as a basic service under the Standard Form of Agreement Between Owner and Architect. You may wish to obtain renderings for use as promotional tools in passing referenda. They can be displayed in the lobby to stimulate public interest and taken to those Rotary club meetings to add a little visual interest while you are plugging your referendum.

✔ Additional services

Your architect can supply you with any number of additional services tailored to your project. Detailed life-cycle cost analyses, models, promotional materials and energy use studies are a few of the potential services you could consider. Another potential service is marketing.

Marketing

At the close of schematic design you will have a reasonably good idea of what your building might look like, how it will work and an indication of its potential cost. In the project checklist presented above, I mentioned the marketing potential of renderings with respect to fund raising. The information collected and the designs generated during schematic design can be powerful marketing tools. People love visual aids. Well chosen renderings can generate excitement for your project. A model of the planned project is always a popular display. Renderings and models can be expensive, but nothing beats them if you need to get your message across in an interesting manner. With computer aided design (CAD), it is now possible to produce startlingly life-like representations of buildings and outdoor spaces for display on a video screen or for reproduction as color photographs. These can even be animated to give the impression of a walk through the still-imaginary building.

The reason that we're discussing marketing now is that the close of the schematic design phase can be a logical point to pause for fund raising. With available cost figures and the potential for some impressive visual presentations, you have a lot more to show than you did at the beginning of the project. Sometimes an institution will retain an architect on a two phase basis. The contract might be written so that the project will proceed beyond the sche-

matic design phase only if the fund-raising effort is successful. In this manner the library is not paying for additional architectural services that it may never need if the funding is not forthcoming. Indeed, if a fully completed architectural project were to sit on the shelf for several years awaiting funding, changes would probably need to be made to the drawings to account for changes in program, equipment and building codes that might have occurred in the interim.

This two phase approach to the architectural project also serves to add a potentially powerful fund raiser to your team—the architect. Architects tend to be involved in their communities. Many of them, due to the nature of their work, are accomplished public speakers. If the board members are making the rounds of the service club lunches, the architect might be asked to come along to help field questions. This gets into the potentially sensitive area of asking the architect to provide what might be pro bono services. If a two phase effort is being considered, discuss this with the architect. He or she might be willing to toss these kinds of appearances in for free, or an hourly rate for these services might be suggested. Either way, the potential for the architect to serve as a salesperson should not be overlooked. After all, they wouldn't have the job if they hadn't sold you.

DESIGN DEVELOPMENT

The goal of design development is to refine and elaborate upon the design that was produced during the schematic design phase. Design development can proceed after the owner has approved and signed off on a schematic design. Now you will begin to see your building take shape. Many of the major decisions may have been made, but there is a lot of input that you, as client, will be expected to provide. It's an exciting time and your building committee will be kept busy in numerous meetings with the architect as design ideas are presented and discussed.

What the architect does

During design development the architect begins to define the details of the project. The structural system, mechanical/electrical systems, and site design are developed. Floor plans are drawn which show spaces and program elements in scale and with the correct relationships. Drawings are developed which illustrate the exterior appearance of the building to a greater level of detail than was generated during the schematic design. On a typical project the design development phase represents approximately 20 percent of the architect's contract.

The outline specification will also be expanded and more selections of materials and types of construction are made. Room finishes and lighting systems will be defined. The board and the library director will want to be familiar with these choices and should take an active part in the selection process. The interior finishes will determine to a large extent the "feel" of your library. The outline specifications will also include general information regarding the electrical and mechanical systems of the building. Again, your building engineer should be involved in the review of all proposed building systems.

At this stage of the project, the architect is actively coordinating the work of numerous consultants who are contributing to the evolution of the building. Scale drawings are produced by the structural, electrical, mechanical and plumbing engineers to insure that the systems for which they are responsible are integrated into the overall building design. A lot of the architect's time goes into the coordination of the consultants. This coordination is essential to insure against time-consuming and potentially costly changes later in the project. The building engineer should be made a part of this process to represent the library and verify that decisions made regarding building systems are consistent with the ideas that were defined in the schematic design.

The set of drawings that the architect has been working on will begin to grow as additional sheets for the structural and mechanical systems are included. Until this point, the layman could probably pick up the drawings and understand pretty much what was being indicated on each sheet. The information that is now being included by the structural and mechanical consultants is more esoteric. Few board members can look at a heating and ventilating sheet, or an electrical drawing and get a real feel for what's going on. As the architect gives you progress sets of drawings, take a little time to review them. Note any questions and don't be afraid to ask them during review meetings. As the advertising slogan goes, "An informed consumer is our best customer." As a trustee of someone else's money, it is your duty to be that "informed consumer."

What the board should do

The board's responsibilities during design development will resemble those of the schematic design phase. Your primary duty is to maintain an active role by frequently reviewing and commenting upon the architect's work. As before, set up a regular series of meetings so the architect may present progress sets showing the progress of the work to date. Be prepared to have a number of special meetings between the architect and the building committee to discuss detailed questions. All decisions made at these meetings should be written and transmitted to the board for review at the next full board meeting.

Goals revisited

As the design development proceeds, review the building goals that were identified back during the programming phase. It is easy to get so involved with the day to day progress of your project that you lose sight of the original goals. They should be dusted off and examined from time to time to verify that the project is evolving in conformance with them. They may have to be revised somewhat in light of what you've learned since then. If so, revise them in a formal manner at a board meeting and record the changes. The degree to which you attain your goals will be one of the yardsticks by which you can evaluate the success of your building and the performance of your architect.

At the close of the design development phase the architect will usually make a presentation to the board to secure formal approval of the material produced. The board should again formally indicate their acceptance by signing off on the work.

What the architect should give you

At the end of the design development phase you will have a complete building design. Floor plans, elevations, site plans and landscape plans will all be drawn to scale. Materials will be indicated and the various structural and mechanical systems will be shown. At the owner's request, a detailed estimate of the construction cost can be produced at this time. I recommend asking the architect to involve a professional cost consultant to help improve the accuracy of the cost estimate.

The design development submittal should include the following documents:

✔ Architectural floor plans

Floor plans should be provided for all areas of the building. The scale of the plans will be larger than that for the schematic design plans. For most buildings the scale should be at least $1/8$"equals one foot. Larger scale ($1/4$" to a foot) detailed plans may be given for areas of particular complexity or importance. Walls should be indicated with their appropriate thicknesses and door swings should be drawn.

The structural grid system should be developed and shown on the plans. The structural grid is a system of intersecting lines which intersect at column locations, this allows each column to be defined by a particular grid position. (e.g. Column A-7). Built-in casework and built-in equipment should also be shown.

✔ Reflected ceiling plans

Reflected ceiling plans show the construction of the ceiling as if it is being looked down upon from above. They will show the layout of ceiling tile grid systems (if any), ceiling details and the locations of light fixtures, ventilation grilles and sprinkler heads.

✔ Interior elevations

Detailed interior elevations will be produced at a later stage. At this point there may only be a few to illustrate some of the more important interior spaces. The interior elevations will illustrate the appearance of doors, windows, casework and other interior detailing. Only built-in items will be shown; moveable equipment and furniture are typically omitted.

✔ Building elevations

Building elevations will be included with finish materials indicated and vertical dimensions shown. Windows and doors should be drawn to represent the appearance of the selected items. The scale of the drawings will usually be the same as that of the floor plans. Roof structures, including mechanical equipment, should be indicated. Larger scale partial elevations should be given for particularly important or complicated areas.

✔ Building sections

Building sections will be shown with greater detail than those given on the schematic design documents. Spaces for ducts should be indicated as should floor levels and suspended ceilings. The building sections are particularly important in enhancing your understanding of the building, and should be studied closely.

✔ Construction details

Some of the more important construction details that will play an important part in establishing the building's character may be included. These may include typical wall sections, parapets, window details, stair details, construction details for interior partitions and custom mill work items.

✔ Site plan

A site plan should show the building placement, parking lots, anticipated site circulation and major landscape features. Easements and rights-of-way should be indicated as should civil engineering items such as sewers, fire hydrants and manholes. The plan should show the proposed grading scheme, landscaping and site lighting plan.

✔ Outline specification

The specification will be developed to a greater degree of detail than for the schematic design phase. Selections for major construction and finish materials should be included.

✔ Estimates of construction cost

The estimated construction cost should be furnished and broken down to show line item costs for various building components such as foundations, structural systems, finishes, plumbing, electrical systems, etc. Sizable contingencies are typically included to cover for unanticipated conditions and changes. The contingencies can be reduced somewhat as the design is developed.

✔ Structural plans and details

A general indication of the structural plan of the building might be included. As with the other consultants, these drawings should be carefully coordinated with the architectural sheets.

✔ Mechanical, electrical and plumbing plans and details

Some information regarding the mechanical, electrical and plumbing systems might be included. These sections will illustrate the construction of their respective systems. Coordination with the architectural sheets is again of primary importance in assuring a successful project.

✔ Renderings

As with schematic design, detailed renderings are not a basic service. Include them in the architect's contract as an extra if you wish.

✔ Additional services

The list of potential additional services is much the same as those we covered in schematic design. Probably the most significant addition would be interior design. Interior furnishings and color selections are not part of the scope of work in the Standard Form of Agreement Between Owner and Architect. Many clients retain the architect to design the interiors; others hire an interior designer. If you decide to hire an interior designer, have several joint meetings with both the architect and the interior designer to insure that the they have the compatible understanding of the project and its goals.

The two checklists presented in this chapter are not intended to be exhaustive or universal. Each project is unique, and each architect is different. If the design development site plan doesn't include site lighting, don't automatically assume that you're getting an inferior product and ask for your money back. If the set is lacking something that you feel is particularly important to your project, you can ask the

architect to add it to the set and delay the formal acceptance of the design development documents until they are done to your satisfaction—up to a point.

Talk softly, but carry a signed contract

If the board rejects an architect's submittal as incomplete and requests additional information, it is important to be sure that the services being requested are included in the architect's scope of work as stated in the Standard Form of Agreement Between Owner and Architect. There are occasional stories of architects providing services at the request of their clients and then, after the fact, submitting an invoice for additional fees for services that were not included in their contract. There are other stories of clients who refuse to pay the architect for services already rendered unless the architect provides additional work at no charge. Both scenarios could represent either unethical behavior or poor communications between the owner and the architect. An architect should always inform the client in writing if services are being requested that will result in a change to the contract amount. A client should always be aware of the scope of services included in the contract and expect to pay more for additional services. Maintaining a good architect/client relationship implies a degree of trust in the professional conduct of both parties.

At the close of the design development phase of your project, the needs and desires of the client have found form in the design of a building. The next phase of the architectural project, construction documents, will transform that design into a manual for the construction of your building.

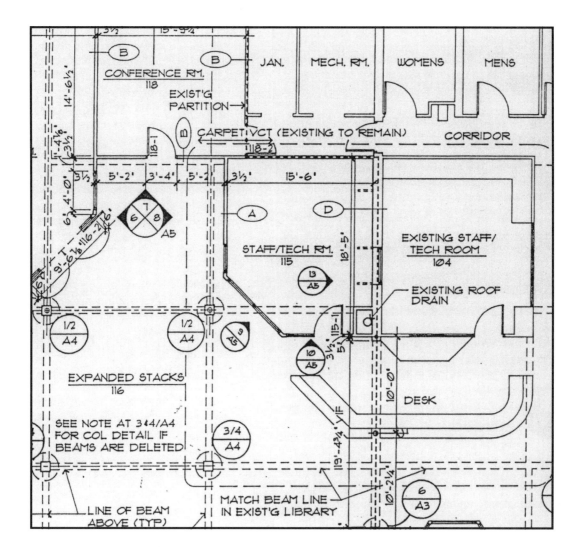

CONFERENCE RM.
118

EXIST'G
PARTITION

JAN. MECH. RM. WOMENS MENS

CARPET : VCT (EXISTING TO REMAIN)   CORRIDOR

STAFF/TECH RM.
115

EXISTING STAFF/
TECH ROOM
104

EXISTING ROOF
DRAIN

EXPANDED STACKS
116

SEE NOTE AT 3 ‡4/A4
FOR COL DETAIL IF
BEAMS ARE DELETED

DESK

LINE OF BEAM
ABOVE (TYP)

MATCH BEAM LINE
IN EXIST'G LIBRARY

8

Construction Documents

God is in the details
Anonymous

In some ways, a building is like a watch. It is an intricate machine comprised of tens-of-thousands of parts. Somewhere, at some time, each of those parts was chosen to satisfy a particular need. The size of every steel bolt was determined by the load it was to carry. The horsepower of each fan motor in the ventilation system was selected by the number of cubic feet of air that it would be expected to push through the ducts in a given time. The paint on the walls was chosen to be resistant to scuffing and have good covering ability. The spacing of the balusters along a stairway is designed so that a child's head will not fit between them.

Windows, beams and bricks

Some of the parts that make up a building move, some are static. Some of them are seen, others hidden. The important point is that they all have to work together. Windows that are fabricated in Iowa must arrive at the site and fit into the openings that the carpenters have made for them; a steel beam from Pennsylvania has to arrive already cut to the proper length and with holes pre-drilled in just the right places so it can take its intended place in the structural frame of the building. Caulk from Illinois has to be delivered in the proper color to match bricks

that are being made in Colorado. Electronic control systems from California must be compatible with rooftop heating units made in Georgia. Thousands of inter-relationships must be worked out and set to paper.

Other kinds of relationships must also be defined. Who is responsible for cleaning up the project site during construction? Who provides the surveys of the site? Who certifies that work is done according to the project specifications before a contractor's request for payment will be honored? Who specifies how much insurance a contractor must carry in order to be able to bid on the work?

A building is like a watch, but only as long as we assume that it is a one-of-a-kind timepiece, made to order for a particular purpose. The written and graphic material that defines the relationships, requirements and set the standards by which the project is to be constructed is known as the construction documents. The preparation of these documents is the responsibility of the architect who, with the assistance of the owner and the architect's consultants, will put together a set of documents which will enable the construction of the building which was planned during design development. A well-prepared set of construction documents answers questions that are likely to come up from any quarter and insures that the building project will, like a good watch, keep on ticking.

What the architect does

The construction documents phase of the project is the most labor intensive and time-consuming phase for the architect. On a typical project the construction documents phase represents approximately 40 percent of the architect's contract. Once the design generated during the design development phase has been approved, the architect can prepare the drawings and specifications that set the requirements for the construction of the project.

The construction drawings show in graphic and written form the extent, design, locations and relationships of the work to be done. Exact dimensions are worked out to insure that the building will "come together." The drawings that the architect puts together will include those described in the last chapter as well as numerous others that are required to adequately describe the building. They will include floor plans, elevations, building sections and site plans, as well as details, diagrams and schedules. During the construction documents phase the architect continues to coordinate the work of the other consultants who have been retained. The consultants will each produce drawings and specifications to a similar level of detail as those produced by the architect. These drawings are assembled into a set which, along with the written specifications, will form the construction documents and will provide contractors with the information that they need to bid and build the project.

As a part of construction documents the project's legal framework is also defined. Contract forms are reviewed with the owner and added to the construction documents package. Information in the contracts, specifications, bid forms and drawings sets forth the legal rights and responsibilities of the owner, the contractor(s) and of the architect. At the end of the construction documents phase the owner will have a complete package of documents which will enable the project to be competitively bid and built.

The architect will have a number of meetings with the client's representatives to make equipment, material and contract decisions. The architect will help guide you in this process by offering advice based on his or her experience.

Dollars and hours

Many clients are startled at the amount of time that goes into a set of construction documents. I've already mentioned that construction documents represent approximately 40 percent of the architect's contract, but how does that translate into hours? And more importantly, what does that mean in dollars?

All projects are different and there is a wide disparity between different architectural firms, and in what architects get paid in different parts of the country. We'll use the drawings portion of the contract documents as an example. In trying to determine fees, some architects use an average of 40 to 60 hours of drawing time to produce a sheet of working drawings. Some sheets have less detail and go quickly, some are complex and take more time. A medium-sized library project might have 20 sheets of architectural drawings. If we use the above average of 50 hours per sheet that translates into 25 full work weeks to produce the architectural drawings alone, not counting additional design time, specifications or all the other sheets that must be produced by the architect's consultants. If you assumed an average billing rate of $50 an hour for an architect, your cost is $50,000 for the architect's portion of the drawings, not including the drawings that will be produced by all the other consultants involved in the project. We will discuss fees in more detail later, but I mention this now to give you an indication of the investment that the architect and the board have in the construction drawings. Also I want to illustrate the importance of having everyone agree on the design development submittal before the architect begins the working drawings. Re-draws can be expensive! Do not take these hourly figures as anything but the broadest of numbers used for the sake of an example. Rates vary enormously and the ever-present effects of inflation also have to be taken into account.

What the architect should give you

The following is a brief description of a set of contract documents. Not every job will have all of the listed items, but it will be helpful as a general outline.

THE CONTRACT DOCUMENTS:

✔ Bidding requirements

The bidding requirements will usually be in five parts. They will usually be on 8½" x 11" sheets and will often be included as a part of the specification.

1. *The Invitation to Bidders:* The document which informs bidders of a project, it may be sent to selected contractors and/or given to contractors who express interest in a project. See chapter eight for an example of an invitation to bidders.

2. *Instructions to Bidders*: This section incorporates by reference a standard AIA document, A701, and gives any modifications to be made to the standard document. See chapter seven for additional information.

3. *Information:* This section will give general project information that will be useful to the bidders. It often takes the form of a project overview.

4. *The Bid Form:* The form which contractors will fill out to indicate the amount of their bid(s). These will be sealed and returned to the library and will usually be opened at a public bid opening.

5. *The Bid Bond:* This form guarantees that the contractor with the low bid will execute the contract at the agreed price within a specified length of time. If the contractor fails to do so, the library will then accept the next-lowest bid and the bonding company will pay the library the difference, usually up to ten percent of the amount of the first contractor's bid.

✔ Contract Forms

The contract forms will usually include the following four sections.

1. *The Agreement:* This is usually AIA document A101, the Standard Form of Agreement Between Owner and Architect, perhaps with modifications as suggested by the client's legal counsel.

2. *The Performance Bond*: This bond guarantees that the contractor will perform the work that he or she has agreed to do. If the contractor fails to maintain the agreement,

the bonding company will provide money to help the library get the work done by another contractor.

3. *The Payment Bond:* This bond guarantees that the contractor will pay the subcontractors that he or she has retained. If the contractor fails to do so, the bonding company will provide money to pay the subcontractors to prevent them from placing liens on the client's property, in this case, the library.

4. *Certificates:* This section is made up of various certificates that the bidding documents require the contractor to furnish to the owner. Many of them are proof-of-insurance certificates.

✔ Contract Conditions

The contract conditions is divided into two parts.

1. *The General Conditions of the Contract:* This document is usually incorporated into the construction documents by reference. It is a standard AIA document which defines the parties to the contract and gives general information regarding the responsibilities of each. It covers many requirements including the contractor's insurance requirements, resolution of disputes between the owner and the contractor, how changes in the contract are to be handled, and how the contractor is to apply for payments. This is a very important document. It defines your rights as the owner and lists your responsibilities. It is important that the library board and the board's legal counsel have a basic understanding of its provisions.

2. *Supplementary Conditions to the Contract:* This document modifies the general conditions of the contract to fit your particular circumstances. As the general conditions is a pre-printed, standard document it cannot fit exactly the requirements of each project. Changes to the general conditions are noted in this section. Public entities often have their own sets of requirements, some of which may contradict those in the general conditions. The supplementary conditions is where these special requirements will be given. The owner's legal counsel will often supply many of these amendments. Other

aspects of the supplementary conditions will be discussed in chapter ten.

✔ Specifications

The specification is a written document which sets the standards of quality for the construction, names products and materials which will be accepted, and itemizes additional responsibilities of the contractor. The specification is customarily divided into 16 sections. The names of many of the sections are enough to describe their contents. I will give some examples where there might be some ambiguity. Each section will contain many subsections, each covering a different product or system.

1. General Requirements: This part sets forth general information relative to your specific project, usually administrative rules and work-related items. It covers things like office procedures, payment and project meetings.

2. Site Work

3. Concrete

4. Masonry

5. Metals

6. Wood and Plastics

7. Thermal and Moisture Protection: Includes insulation and caulk

8. Doors and Windows

9. Finishes

10. Specialties: Varied items, including chalkboards, computer access floors and toilet accessories

11. Equipment: Includes special library equipment and kitchen equipment.

12. Furnishings

13. Special Construction: This section is used in few library projects, it includes special sound controlled rooms, saunas and whirlpools.

14. Conveying Systems: Includes elevators and dumbwaiters

15. Mechanical: Ductwork, furnaces, chillers and ventilation systems

16. Electrical

✔ Drawings

The drawings might consist of just several sheets for a small, interior remodeling project or run to over a hundred sheets for a larger, new building.

The drawings will be divided into groups, the major ones being architectural drawings, structural drawings, mechanical drawings, plumbing drawings and electrical drawings. Smaller, more specialized sections may be included for things like kitchen equipment or specialties like circulation desks and library equipment.

The drawings will also contain schedules for things that are more appropriately presented in a tabular format. These might include door types, room finishes or hardware. It is difficult for the layperson to evaluate the completeness and accuracy of a set of drawings. It's relatively easy for the non-architect to look at some floor plans and get a basic understanding of what they represent. The future occupant can usually even find the answer to the most pressing question of all, namely "How big is my office and does it have any windows?" But things get a little more difficult when it comes to judging a wall section for its insulation value, or determining if a flashing detail will really keep the water out. That is the point when the client must rely on the expertise of the architect. The only real evaluations of the drawings can be done during the construction process, when you see if the project is proceeding smoothly, and after you move in, when you see how well the building really works.

What the board should do

We've already touched on some of the owner's duties during the construction documents phase. Here in more detail are some of the most important ones.

Review the documents

Review the documents with the architect several times during the construction documents phase. Keep current with the drawings as they evolve, for the architect will ask for your input at many points along the way. Selections of carpeting, toilet fixtures, door hardware, casework and a hundred other items will need your approval. The architect will be showing you catalog illustrations of many of the items being proposed for your building along with relative costs. Allow the building committee to make decisions regarding smaller items and have the architect present the major ones to the full board for consideration.

Get a lawyer involved

The board should have the library's legal counsel review all contract documents, especially the general conditions and the owner/contractor agreement and suggest changes that he or she thinks are in the best interest of the library. Any contract changes should be discussed and coordinated with the architect.

Insurance and accounting

The owner is responsible for providing insurance and accounting services as required to build the project. Your insurance agent and attorney can help you with the appropriate amounts and types of insurance.

Ask the engineer

Have your building engineer review designs and selections for the mechanical, electrical and plumbing systems. He or she should verify that the systems selected are realistic and can be maintained by your staff. The maintenance staff should also be asked for their input on finishes and floor coverings that they will be expected to maintain.

Governmental approvals & permits

In the standard owner/architect arrangements, it is the responsibility of the owner to submit the appropriate documents for the approval of the various governmental agencies that insist on having a say in your building project. Some of the permits are relatively obvious like building permits, while some are less well known. A few of the other agencies that you might need to obtain permits from include the city zoning board, the local sanitary district, the Environmental Protection Agency, and the State Department of Transportation. There are others that may be required depending on your local and state requirements.

It may seem that you're wandering into a labyrinth of seemingly unrelated bureaucracies. Fortunately, your architect and the other consultants have found their way through this maze many times, and can help you in preparing and submitting your documentation. Although the burden is on the owner to file the documents,

the architect will customarily lend you assistance. Ask your architect to put together a list of all the applicable permits, along with estimates of the time that it will take for each governmental agency to process the paperwork. Keep this as a checklist for both the board and the architect and cover the subject of permits at each project meeting to track the process and insure that none have been overlooked.

Sign-off

Once again, the board should formally accept the construction documents and sign-off on a reference set that will be retained by the library, and on one that the architect will keep. Dust off the project goals that were established during programming phase and make a final review of the documents to verify that the project goals have been met. If some have not been met, it may be due to budget or other unavoidable limitations. Some of the goals may have changed during the course of the project. If you have been keeping good records, all changes in the project goals should have been noted as they were made. Good record-keeping is important in charting the progress of your project.

A bit of advice

At the end of the construction document phase the architect will usually turn over several sets of the drawings and the specifications to the owner. Usually these will be in the form of prints made from the architect's original drawings. When forming your agreement with the architect, ask that the library be given reproducible copies of the drawings. Prints from the original drawings are reproducible only by the xerographic process. As they age, the prints tend to fade and yellow which reduces the quality of the Xerox prints that might be made from them. If the library has a reproducible set of drawings, it is always certain that additional sheets can be printed should they be needed for reference in the future. The most common reproducible types of drawings are what is called "sepia" prints, and "mylar sepia" prints. Of these two, the mylar sepia will last the longest and is the most suited for a permanent record. They can be expensive, and it will be up to the board members to determine if they feel that the cost is justified. If your project was produced on a computer aided design system, the record drawings can be easily transferred to a few floppy disks which could be stored in the library's bank box.

The reason for my concern about reproducible drawings is based on a personal experience. I was recently involved on a project at a community college where they wished to do a large addition to an existing building. The existing building was only about 20 years old but the college's set of the working drawings had been separated and lost. There's always someone who wants to borrow a set of building drawings—electricians might need to trace existing circuits, plumbers need to find valves, other architects doing remodeling work need the drawings to verify structural details. Unless an iron-willed building engineer takes responsibility for getting the drawings back, it is often just a matter of time before your set is incomplete or missing.

On this particular project, only a few of the prints were still in the hands of the college. The architects who had done the original project had gone out of business several years after doing the school project and had consigned all of their original drawings to a storage shed. Eventually, the original drawings were discarded along with any hope of ever determining exactly how the college's building was put together.

If you get a reproducible copy of your documents, keep them in a safe place away from the possibility of fire or water damage. You probably paid a good sum of money for these documents, so treat them as the investment that they are. You must remember, however, that according to the standard owner/architect contract, the original drawings and the design remain the property of the architect and cannot be reused without permission.

And on with the show

With your construction documents in-hand, you are ready to begin the exciting and frustrating process of getting your building or addition built. In the next chapter we'll take a look at how you go about bidding your project, and I will give you some tips to help guide you through what can be a confusing array of regulations and requirements.

9
Bidding and Negotiation

By the time that a building is bid, the architect and the owner have invested a large amount of their time, energy and money in the project. When the drawings "hit the street" the architect feels something like a parent whose child is going out into the world. The product that you have slaved over, worried about, and nurtured is, for the first time, going to be exposed to the scrutiny and the judgment of others. Like a new parent, we tend to have a lot of pride in what we have produced. When the contractors' calls and questions start coming in, the architect is brought suddenly back to earth and the work resumes. Sometimes the questions are tactfully presented. "Did you really mean to specify the gold-plated plumbing fixtures for the library director's washroom? It looks like it might be a typing error in the specification." At least this one leaves an easy way out. Sometimes the questions are honed to a slightly finer edge. "Are you sure that you want to put this kind of finish on the wood doors? You know what that'll look like in a few months, don't you?" Then there is the occasional "How can you expect anybody to build this?" Every project needs its measure of clarifications and adjustments before it can be built. During the bidding phase one of the architect's prime jobs is to iron out these rough spots and keep things running as smoothly as possible.

The culmination of the bidding process is, of course, the opening of the bids. That is the moment of truth, for all the cards are on the table. The desired outcome is a good number of consistent bids that fall comfortably within the project budget. Things are seldom so simple in real life, but with a little luck, and some good planning, we can usually avoid scenarios like the one described for the fictional re-roofing project in chapter three. Even assuming good planning, the bids for a building project are influenced by numerous forces, many of them out of the control of the architect and the owner. Some of the variables are the local labor rates and the timing of the project with respect to the workload of the local contractors—in other words, the laws of supply and demand. The quality of the construction documents, unusual requirements requested by the owner and the time allotted for the construction of the project will also influence the outcome of the bidding.

The mechanics of the bidding process should be understood by both the library representatives and the architect. For public work it is vitally important the standard procedures be followed and that everything is in conformance with local and state regulations. Any irregularities could result in a legal challenge to your bids, potentially resulting in costly delays to your project. Be prepared to spend some time working with your architect and the library's legal counsel to guarantee that everything has been properly prepared. In a Standard Owner/

Architect Contract the bidding phase represents approximately five percent of the architect's fee.

Before we go into the particulars of the bidding process, let's take a look at a few of the different ways that a project can be bid and what they might mean to you.

Project options

There are two basic ways that a building project can be designed and bid. The first is by separate contracts for design and construction; the second is a single contract for design and construction. Each method has its own advantages and drawbacks.

Separate Contracts for Design and Construction (The conventional method)

The separate contract method is the most common way of bidding and constructing a building. For public work, many states require that this method be used. With separate contracts, the owner hires an architect and a contractor and has a separate contract with each of them. The process has a defined sequence; the architect is hired first to produce a set of documents which enables the building to be bid. The contractor is then selected and hired based on the results of the bidding. This book is largely based on the assumption that you will use separate contracts for your project. After the project is bid and the contract is let, the architect will function as your representative, administering the construction contract and helping to insure that the contractor's work is in accordance with the drawings and the specifications.

There are a number of advantages with this arrangement. The primary one is that you, representing the owner, are intimately involved in the decisions made during the design and programming phases. The nature of your involvement in the process has been the subject of the previous chapters in this book. Another advantage is that, because of the architect's ongoing price estimates, you should have a good idea of the eventual cost of your project. This leads us to a variation of this method—the "fast-track" approach.

When a project has unusual time constraints, such as a requirement to vacate your existing building by a certain date, it might be necessary to take measures to expedite the construction process as much as possible. This is the purpose of fast-track construction. "Fast-tracking" a project refers to beginning construction before the drawings and specifications are fully complete. The design for the entire building might be taken as far as the design development phase at which time the architect turns his or her attention to the parts of the project that would be done first during construction. Thus, the architect would turn out detailed foundation and structural drawings and specifications before refining the rest of the design. As construction work begins on those parts of the project, the rest of the building design is completed.

You can probably imagine that this method entails a number of risks. First, as the building design isn't complete, you will have a less refined rough estimate of the final construction cost of the building when construction begins. Added to that, changes to the design become increasingly difficult as the foundations already in the ground begin to fix the size and configuration of the building. If previously poured foundations have to be removed and relocated due to design changes, you begin to lose the time advantage of the fast-track method, in addition to paying twice for the foundations. Lastly, fast-tracking depends on a high degree of coordination, cooperation and expertise on the part of the contractor, architect and owner. Such projects require expert management to be brought off successfully. All in all, you should always consider any other options available to you before considering fast-track construction.

A Single Contract for Design and Construction

The popular term for this method of construction is "design/build." With this type of contract the owner hires a single firm to design and build the project. The typical design/build firm has both architects and contractors on staff who work together to produce your project. The primary advantage to you is that, under this system, the design/build firm offers you a single source of responsibility for all aspects of the project.

There are several disadvantages to design/build. During the construction phase of a conventional (separate contract) project, the architect is working directly for the owner. He or she is there to represent you and to protect your interests. With the design/build system, the architect works for the design/build company, not for the owner. This carries the implication that, in a dispute between a contractor and the owner, the concerns of the owner might not be adequately represented. In addition, the design/build firm is vested with the responsibility of bringing in the project on time and within the budget. That sounds good, but the other side of the equation is that the design/build firm has the authority, to a degree, to make changes in the project to insure that the time and budget criteria are met. This can tend to reduce the owner's input in the decision-making process. Because of the potential conflict of interest, the AIA for many years prohibited architects from participating in design/build arrangements. The prohibition was reconsidered in 1978, and design/build was incorporated into the AIA's revised code of ethics in 1987.

Public work usually must be constructed using separate contracts for design and construction. This is due, in part, to the requirements that most states have concerning the necessity of obtaining competitive bids for work of any significant size. The library board should always consult the library's legal counsel if it is considering using a design/build firm.

BIDDING

We begin this section assuming that the architect, working with the client, has produced a complete set of construction documents. Many of the documents involved, drawings and specifications, have been described in the previous chapters of this book. A portion of the construction documents will be devoted to the conditions and requirements of the bidding process. Some of these documents will usually be included as a portion of the specification. Let's look at several bidding documents and identify some things that should be included and some of the decisions that the architect and the owner must make.

The advertisement for bids

Most states require that, for public work, an advertisement for bids be published in a local and/or state newspaper and a building trade publication. Check with your legal counsel for the requirements in your area. Please refer to appendix II for a sample advertisement for bids that illustrates some of the information that you should consider including.

The instructions to bidders

The next part of the bidding documents is the "Instructions to Bidders." This section incorporates by reference a standard AIA document, A701, and gives any modifications to be made to the standard document. Its purpose is to instruct the bidders on the general bidding requirements for a project and to define terms to help prevent ambiguity in the project documents. It states that each bidder, by submitting a bid, has declared that he or she understands the bidding documents and has become familiar with local conditions as required to be a responsible bidder.

As some of the text makes reference to responsibilities of the owner and to the owner's financial capabilities, you should read the material in the instructions to bidders to insure that you understand the library's obligations.

Other sections of the instructions to bidders cover the interpretation of and corrections to the bidding documents, substitutions to items specified in the bidding documents, bidding procedures and bond requirements. Discuss this section with your architect if you have any questions as to whether or not all the sections are applicable to you, or if local regulations require changes to the standard form. Changes to the standard language will be made in a separate section entitled "Supplementary Instructions to Bidders." Review this document to verify that it is consistent with your understanding of any changes that you have discussed with the architect.

The bid form

One or more copies of the bid form are usually distributed to each prospective bidder, and an additional copy is often included in the front of the specification. Bids are customarily presented in sealed envelopes. For public work they are usually required to be opened at a public meeting and the bid amounts read aloud. The architect will customarily prepare the bid form. As always, check with the library's attorney to verify that everything is in conformance with local regulations.

Owner requested alternates

When putting together the bid form, the owner and the architect may decide that it could be advantageous to include one or more parts of the work as owner-requested alternates. The purpose of alternates is often to try to insure that the bids for the major part of the work will fall within the project budget. Portions of the work that may push the project over budget, or that the board feels might cost more than they are worth to the library, are listed separately. The library board can decide later whether or not to include those parts of the work in the contract for construction. If properly selected, alternates will help reduce the potential of all the bids coming in over the project budget, thus avoiding a potential re-bid of the project. The cost breakdown that alternates provide also gives the board the chance to evaluate the costs of the selected portions of the work.

As an example, let's assume the following:

A. The project construction budget is $3,000,000. This does not include a standing-seam metal roof for the main building and an outdoor story area for the children's library. For the "base bid" an asphalt shingle roof has been indicated and the story area has been omitted.

B. The architect's estimate for the building without the standing-seam metal roof or story area is $2,900,000. The metal roof has been designated as "Alternate #1" and the story area as "Alternate #2."

C. When the bids are received the lowest bid for the base bid work (*No metal roof for story area.*) is $2,850,000.

D. The bidder with the above cost has bid $200,000 for the inclusion of the metal roof.

E. That same bidder has bid $100,000 to include the story area.

We can immediately see the advantage of breaking those two items out of the base bid. If they had not been pulled out as separate items the bid for the project would have been: $2,850,000 + $200,000 + $100,000, giving a total of $3,250,000 which is well over the project budget. If additional funds were not available, the only recourse would have been for the library to have the architect re-design parts of the project and re-bid it in the hope that it would come within the budget. This would be expensive for the library and could disrupt the construction schedule.

With the alternates, however, there is a recourse. The library could elect not to accept the alternate bids and proceed only with the base bid work. In this case, the contractor could be selected, hired and the work could begin. The alternate bid for the metal roof would put the total cost at $3,050,000, which is over the project budget. The obvious question is: "Couldn't we accept the base bid work and the second alternate bid and at least get the story area?" This would give a total of $2,950,000, which is $50,000 under the limit. The answer is "Maybe not." If your library is a public library, some states will require that the alternates be listed in order of preference and only accepted in that order. In this case, the cost for the metal roof put the project over budget and you are not allowed to go on to the next alternate.

The rationale for this rule is that, by picking and choosing alternates, it would be possible to come up with a number of different "low bidders" depending on which alternates were selected. It would therefore be possible to steer the work to a favored contractor by juggling alternates. In most states, this kind of bid manipulation is illegal for public work. For private libraries however, this rule often does not apply and the owner is free to select different combinations of alternates at will. For a large, complex project with lots of alternate bids, the process of selecting the "low bidder" can become very involved. In this case, the architect will often prepare a number of different combinations involving different alternates and present them to the board for a decision. This process is usually called "bid analysis."

Addenda

After the bidding documents are released to the public, the contractors begin to assemble their prices for the work. Costs are investigated and hours are estimated. During this period many questions and requests for clarifications will crop up. The architect will spend a lot of time on the phone responding to contractors' questions. To avoid any inequality in the bidding, any clarification or change that might result in a change to the bid amounts will be issued to all the plan holders in the form of an addendum.

Addenda, when released, become a part of the bidding documents and carry the same authority as any of the drawings or specifications. There are often legal limits on how close to bidding time that addenda can be issued. Legalities aside, three days is often considered to be a minimum amount of time. A week would be better. General contractors may have to seek additional price information from suppliers due to changes required by an addendum, this process can take several days to accomplish.

Addenda are often issued in an $8\frac{1}{2}$" x 11" format to allow them to be attached to the written project specifications. Now that we've covered some of the bidding documents, let's look at an overview of the bidding procedure and you will see where these documents fit into the process.

The bidding process

Listed below is the step-by-step procedure for bidding your project. These steps will apply to most projects, although modifications may be required to suit your circumstances and conform with local regulations.

✔ Publish the advertisement

When the advertisement for bids and the bid forms have been written, the process of bidding the project can begin. As the owner, the first step is to publish the advertisement for bids. The timing and place for the publication will usually be determined by state law. The advertisement is often required to be first published anywhere from two to five weeks before the date of the planned bid opening.

Contractors whom the library board is particularly interested in working with may be contacted directly and asked to submit a bid on the project. This is allowable as long as they are given no preferential treatment. An example of preferential treatment in this case might be giving the bidding documents to a desired bidder before they are generally available to other bidders.

✔ Prequalification of bidders (Optional)

Contractors may be asked to prove that they are qualified and capable of doing the work described in the bidding documents. This can occur either before or after the bids are taken. Sometimes public bodies may have lists of "prequalified" contractors who have already been investigated and approved. The problem with this form of pre-qualification is that the lists often do not get updated. A contractor who

may have been in fine financial shape when the list was drawn up could now be having difficulties which might jeopardize your project. The prequalification list might also have been assembled for a different kind of project than the one you are now undertaking. For example, a contractor deemed suitable for building a 2000 square foot addition might not be the appropriate choice for building a new library at 70,000 square feet. For these reasons, I recommend that prequalification be done on a project-by-project basis.

Sometimes contractors are required to become prequalified with the public body before they are allowed to obtain sets of bidding documents. This effectively limits the bidders to firms that have been prequalified and approved. An advantage to prequalification before bidding is that time will not be wasted in evaluating bids which may later be disallowed if the contractor cannot meet the conditions of qualification. The disadvantage of prequalification is that much more time is spent up front in evaluating each firm that wants to pick up drawings. If the architect is to do the prequalification screening, the time involved might not be included in the owner/architect contract. If not, the architect might be due additional fees.

In prequalifying bidders, there are several standard questions. The first thing to check is that the contractor has successfully built projects of comparable size and complexity. Secondly, the general financial condition of the contractor should be evaluated to determine that the company can live up to the cash flow requirement of your size of project. Quality of past work should also be considered. Speak to architects and owners who have worked with the contractor before and get their opinions. This is a subjective measurement, however, and must be considered in that light. Lastly, inquire about the bonding capacity of the contractor. If a surety company has investigated the contractor and approved the firm for bonding, it is an indication that the contractor is financially solvent.

The American Institute of Architects has a standard form, "Contractor's Qualification Statement" (AIA Document A305), which is intended to assist the owner and the architect in screening contractors. It covers all the above material as well as a number of additional items that will help you in your evaluation of contractors. As with most other aspects of the bidding procedure, you should confirm the legality of prequalification with the library's legal counsel as laws regulating bidding will vary from state to state.

✔ The pre-bid conference

Several weeks before the bids are due, a meeting should be arranged at the project site to enable potential bidders to ask questions regarding the project. If there is no suitable place at the project site, the meeting could take place in a conference room at the library. The architect must be in attendance, as should several members of the building committee. Careful minutes of the meeting should be kept and an attendance sheet should be passed around. The architect will usually keep the meeting minutes. Proof of attendance could be important in the event of a future dispute with a contractor regarding the work. Copies of the minutes should be distributed to all potential bidders and be included with any drawing sets that might be subsequently distributed. The date and location of the meeting should be included in the original bidding documents to insure that all plan holders are duly informed of it. Any potential changes to the scope or content of the project documents should be noted in the meeting minutes. Any significant changes will be issued in the form of one or more addenda to the construction documents.

✔ Issue addenda

If changes that are required to be made to the project documents, the architect will prepare addenda that will itemize the modifications to the construction documents. These will usually be in the form of 81/2" x 11" sheets. These changes may be the result of the pre-construction meeting, or from questions telephoned to the architect during the bidding period.

Because an addendum changes the scope of the work, there should always be a meeting between the architect and the building committee to insure that there is a consensus on the form and content of an addendum before it is released to the bidders. As an addendum is in effect a contract document, the building committee should sign-off on it prior to its issuance. Due to the time constraints of the bidding

period, the building committee should be prepared to meet promptly to review addenda. Addenda should always be issued as far in advance of the bid opening as possible.

✔ Open the bids

When the date arrives for the opening of the bids, make certain that there is someone in the office to receive them as they are delivered. Check the accuracy of the library clock beforehand to insure that you know when the deadline has passed. A measure like this might seem a bit over cautious, but considering the expense and effort that has to go into a re-bid, it is worth spending a little extra effort up front.

At the appointed hour, a representative from the library should carry the bids to the room in which the opening is to take place and make an announcement that an open meeting has been called for the purpose of opening the bids. The official name of the project should be stated.

The sealed envelopes should be opened one at a time. The person reading the bids should publicly state the following:

The name of the bidder

The amount of the base bid

The amounts of any alternate bids, in the order presented on the bid form

Whether or not the bidder has acknowledged receipt of addenda

The amount of the bid security enclosed with the bid

A general statement confirming that the bid appears to be in order (i.e. there are no additional notes, conditions or other irregularities attached to the bid form).

When all the bids have been opened and read, the person should thank any persons in attendance and close the public meeting. No interpretations of the bids should be offered as the low bidder cannot be determined until the bids have been properly analyzed.

✔ Analyze the bids

Until the bids have been analyzed, the bidder with the lowest total bid is only the "apparent" low bidder. Alternates to the base bid must be examined and selected. Each bid form must be thoroughly scrutinized to determine if the bid is acceptable. If the bidders were required to submit statements of qualification, the architect will first verify that the apparent low bidder is qualified according to the predetermined standards set by the library board. The bid security is verified and, if it is in the form of a bond, the bonding company is investigated to insure that its rating conforms with any requirements listed in the project documents. For public work, it is sometimes required that bids with any "irregularities" such as additional notes attached by the contractor to the bid forms be disallowed.

If there are a number of bids, it is customary to promptly return the bid securities to all the bidders except the lowest three or four bidders. For many projects, the bid security can be in the form of a certified check. Unsuccessful bidders are understandably anxious to have them back. After a successful bidder has been selected and a contract signed, the remaining bid securities are usually returned.

✔ Signing the contract

When the successful bidder has been selected, the contract can be signed. The usual form will be one of the AIA standard contracts, in this case AIA document A101, "The Standard Form of Agreement Between Owner and Contractor." Some governmental agencies and large corporations prefer to write their own owner/contractor contract. Federal and state government usually have their own forms. For the great majority of users however, it makes sense to use the AIA contracts.

Since the turn-of-the-century, the American Institute of Architects has been developing a large number of standardized contracts and forms. They have been developed with the benefit of years of experience and have clauses and will address most situations likely to come up during a construction project. The standard contracts are intended to reflect a consensus of organizations involved in the construction industry and attempt to remain unbiased toward any party. Considering the resources afforded by the standard documents, I would recommend against asking your legal counsel to write a custom contract for an architectural project. It is not, however, unusual for an owner's attorney to modify one of the standard contracts to satisfy the particular requirements of a project.

This is almost always the option preferred to writing a custom contract.

Schedule a meeting with the chosen contractor, the architect, representatives of the building committee, and perhaps the library's attorney, for the signing of the contract. Take this meeting as an opportunity to discuss the project with the contractor and allow him or her to bring up potential problems or opportunities from the point of view of the person responsible for constructing the project. The contractor will often come up with ideas for improving the project or expediting the work.

After the contract is signed, return the remaining bid securities to the unsuccessful bidders. As a courtesy, I usually enclose a brief note thanking them for their time and effort. Assembling a bid for a project of any magnitude is no small task, and a little recognition for their efforts is usually appreciated.

The birth of a building

With a signed contract in hand, you are about to embark on an adventure. Nearly every day will bring a new challenge—some of them will be welcome opportunities, and others will require some difficult negotiations to sort out. Be prepared to devote a lot of your time and energy to the construction phase of your project. If you can keep the right attitude and regard the process as an adventure rather than a burden, you will find that you're able to relax more and enjoy it. It's not every day that you get the chance to attend the birth of a building!

10

Construction Administration

The beginnings and endings of all human undertakings are untidy, the building of a house, the writing of a novel, the demolition of a bridge, and, eminently, the finish of a voyage. **Galsworthy**

Things are always at their best in the beginning. **Pascal**

An untidy optimism

There's nothing like the start of a building project. The inevitable problems in making a building come together have yet to surface and everything is still on schedule. It is an exciting time.

There is an untidy optimism as the contractor's forces are assembled on the site. Backhoes and earthmovers are marshalled in ragged lines. Piles of drain tile, concrete forms, rolls of fencing and plastic sheeting are scattered in seeming disarray. Portable toilets, set on uneven ground and leaning at uncomfortable angles, guard the flanks. In contrast to the apparent confusion, surveyor's stakes, in precise rows, neatly trace the outline of what will someday be a library.

Flashbulbs and gold shovels

One of the most memorable events of the long process of building a new library, or of adding

an addition, is the ground breaking. The ceremonial first shovelfuls of earth are dug, cameras click, flashes flash, maybe a speech is made and then the party breaks up. The local newspaper might have photographs of a smiling group, each person holding a gold-plated shovel. The casual newspaper reader, pausing at the photograph, will usually have little idea of the amount of time and effort that the team has expended to get the project this far. The team members themselves may underestimate the amount of time and effort that it's going to take to finish this trip. Much remains to be done, many lessons will be learned and many decisions will be made before the keys to a new building are handed over. In this chapter, we will look at the construction process, what you should do, what you should know and what you should expect.

A commercial break

Being a memorable event, the ground breaking should be utilized for all its inherent publicity value. Good public relations is important for any tax-supported institution, and we should always look for opportunities to increase public involvement in the library. The construction phase offers some good opportunities for media exposure. Some frequent library users could be invited to participate in the ground breaking. Get your state senator or representative to lay the first brick. Cornerstones with time capsules offer a golden opportunity to stimulate some public interest. Contests might be held at different levels of the local schools to select the contents of the capsule. See if the local Kiwanis club will donate and plant the first tree when it's time put in the landscaping. If there's a local garden club, see if the members will take over the design and maintenance of one or two of the flower beds. Wring it out for all it's worth and insist that the local newspaper cover everything. If your funding comes from referenda and property levies, you owe it to the taxpayers to show them what their money is buying and to give them a feeling of involvement with their new library.

THE PROJECT TEAM

During the construction phase of the project, the composition of your project team will change and the roles of the players will be somewhat altered. The involvement of the library staff will diminish as the design that they helped to shape moves into the construction phase. The library director and the building engineer should continue to offer their input during the construction phase as many questions will come up that they will be best qualified to answer.

During this time the role of the architect will also change, he or she will take on some new responsibilities in order to get your building built. We looked at the nature of the architect/owner relationship back in chapter three. The agency relationship, where the architect is empowered to act on behalf of the owner, is most pronounced during the construction phase of the building project. The architect will be making many decisions which are binding on you, as the owner. Contractor's pay requests will be authorized, judgements will be rendered on the acceptability of the contractors' work, meetings will be scheduled and shop drawings reviewed. For the architect, construction contract administration is a time-consuming task. In a standard contract, it comprises approximately 20 percent of the architect's fee.

Remember also, that the architect may be required to act as an impartial arbiter in the event of disputes between the owner and the contractor. That is where the nature of the services offered by the architect is a little different than that of other professionals that you know of. You pay an attorney to remain strictly "on

your side" no matter what. Your case might be groundless and your judgement faulty, but you know that your lawyer is going to back you up. You pay an architect, on the other hand, not only to represent you, but also to get a building built. On certain occasions during construction, those two roles can come into conflict. This is especially true in the case of disagreements between the owner and the contractor. On those occasions, the architect is required by the construction contract to render an impartial decision consistent with the terms of the contract between the owner and the contractor. While somewhat unusual, this concept has been time-tested and has been shown to be an effective way to get your building built.

This role seldom results in an adversarial relationship between the owner and the architect. In the final analysis, the owner controls the purse strings and has final say on the disbursement of the funds. If you found yourself in some irreconcilable disagreement with your architect regarding a conflict with the contractor, it would be possible to terminate the architect's contract, pay him or her for the services to date and to try to find a different architect who will see things your way. Meanwhile, there is a new character who might be involved in your project, and who is always in your corner.

The clerk of the works

For an institution that is controlled by a board of directors, like many libraries, it can be difficult to assemble the group each time a quick decision is required. In addition, the library director usually has enough to do without having to give constant attention to the building project. In this case, the board might decide to retain a "clerk of the works." The clerk of the works is a person who represents and acts on the behalf of the owner at the job site. This person can relieve the library director and the board of many of the mundane, day-to-day tasks that must be addressed while the building is being built and take over many of the routine interactions with the architect and the contractor. In addition, if the person is experienced in the construction of buildings, he or she will be a valuable asset to the project.

Great care should be exercised in selecting a clerk of the works. Giving the task to the wrong individual could have serious repercussions and disrupt the delicate balance of the relationships between the owner, contractor and architect. I advise that you look for an individual who stresses cooperation rather than an individual who bills him or herself as a "junkyard dog," and guarantees to settle every dispute to the owner's advantage. Some of the primary qualifications might be a thorough knowledge of construction and an even disposition. Sometimes, a retired contractor or architect might be the appropriate choice.

Ask other institutions in your area that have built recently if they had a clerk of the works. Your state library might be also be able to steer you toward qualified individuals. The clerk of the works is a strictly optional position. Discuss the concept with the library director and amongst the board to see if there is a consensus as to whether or not a clerk of the works might be required for your project.

If you elect to hire a clerk of the works, the board should first meet and decide exactly how much authority will be vested in this individual. The job description should be worked out in detail to reduce the potential for confusion later. Your architect might be able to assist you in identifying potential assignments and in determining the scope of the clerk's responsibilities.

The chain of command

As during the design phase, the library board should establish a chain of command for dealing with changes, adjustments and minor emergencies during construction. Items which involve a significant adjustment to the cost of the construction contract or a change in the estimated completion date should always be brought before the board of directors for discussion and approval. Other individuals involved in the project should be empowered to make decisions regarding items which do not affect the contract. You should decide who is empowered to make the decisions, and define the limits of their responsibility. The typical chain of responsibility for problem resolution would start with the clerk of the works, move up to the library director, then to the building committee and end with the full board of directors. Just how far a particular type of problem should move up this ladder of responsibility should be defined at the start of the project. The architect is, of course, available at all points of this process to lend assistance.

The project representative

In addition to, or as an alternate to employing a clerk of the works, the architect can supply a project representative. This should be considered for fast track jobs and other projects of particular complexity. A full-time project representative is not included in the standard owner/architect contract and is usually billed as an additional service. A project representative performs many of the same services that the architect provides, but gives the advantage of a quick turn-around time and nearly continuous job site observation.

It's important that the owner realizes that the standard owner/architect contract does not make the architect responsible for continual or exhaustive on-site observation. If you feel that your project calls for this kind of attention, discuss the options with your architect.

CONSTRUCTION

I always look forward to hearing individual reactions to a new building when it begins to take shape. "It's so much (bigger, smaller, taller, shorter, brighter, dimmer, harder, softer, more impressive, more understated, better, worse, redder, bluer, greener....) than I thought it was going to be." The average person is not accustomed to reading plans, and the finished product is usually something of a revelation. It also happens to the architect. We usually have a better idea than anyone else just what the building is going to look like, but there are always surprises. Some of them are pleasant. We might never have realized how good of a job we did in integrating the building into the neighborhood context, and while patting ourselves on the back, we notice that something like the rooftop ventilating units have a lot more prominence than we ever intended.

Every job will have its share of surprises. With a little study, you can acquaint yourself with the general game plan of a construction project. This won't eliminate the unexpected, but it might make you better prepared to deal with it when it comes. In this chapter, we will take a look at some of the highlights of the of a typical construction project.

Early in this book I spoke of the need for a common language between the architect and the owner. Think of this chapter as a kind of grammar lesson where we will learn some of the rules by which buildings are built. Our aim is to insure that you will have the same understanding as your architect of some of the more important concepts. Every project is different, but much of what follows should apply to your situation.

Ground rules

When a contract for construction has been awarded, one of the first orders of business will be to hold a meeting to set the ground rules for the project. With a little effort, this meeting can set a precedent for effective communication between all the players during construction.

The preconstruction meeting

Before the ground breaking ceremony, there is much that must be done. After the successful bidder has been determined, a preconstruction meeting will be scheduled. The architect will usually prepare the agenda and run the meeting. Here are some of the major items that should be on the agenda in the preconstruction meeting.

☑ Introductions

Everyone who will be involved in project management should be introduced and his or her responsibilities detailed. The architect or the contractor should be instructed to prepare a project directory which gives the names and phone numbers of each individual with management responsibilities. Identify the people who should be contacted in case of emergency.

☑ The notice to proceed

The contractor should be given a formal, signed notice to proceed. This is issued and signed by the owner. The notice establishes the official date of the beginning of construction. The general conditions state that the contractor may begin work upon receipt of the notice. If a set amount of time has been set by contract for the construction of the building, the clock begins ticking upon the contractor's receipt of the notice to proceed.

☑ The general and supplementary conditions of the contract

During the preconstruction meeting the architect should review the general and supplementary conditions of the project documents with the contractor and the owner's representative.

These documents will contain information which will govern much of the day-to-day administration of the construction project. They also define the responsibilities of the owner and of the contractor. Some of the items on this checklist are drawn from provisions in the general and supplementary conditions.

☑ Schedule and provisions for payments to the contractor

The procedure and timing for payments to the contractor should be discussed. Before each payout, there are specific things that the contractor must provide and that the owner and the architect much do. These are defined in the general conditions of the contract. All parties should review the requirements to insure that everyone understands the procedures. At each pay request, the architect will certify that the contractor has completed all the work for which he or she is billing.

☑ Project schedule

A project schedule should be established and milestone dates should be set for significant construction events. These dates are helpful for following the progress of the work. Keep in mind that, no matter how pressing your project schedule, there are many things that can disrupt the most carefully laid plans. Many of them are out of the control of the contractor, such as bad weather, labor strikes and unforeseen site conditions.

☑ Project meetings

A schedule and format for project meetings should be established, along with a minimum agenda. Meetings may occur only at payouts or might be held more frequently, depending on circumstances. The person responsible for keeping and distributing meeting minutes should be named as should the representatives who will be attending the meetings.

☑ Miscellaneous

Before the preconstruction meeting, the board staff representatives should meet and make a list of items that are of special concern to the library. The list could form part of the agenda for the preconstruction meeting. Items on this list might include the contractor's access to the site, the use of library washrooms and phones by the contractor's personnel, parking, and site clean-up. Many of these items will also be covered in the general conditions to the contract. Contractors' personnel will have varying degrees of familiarity with the general conditions, it never hurts to review the ones that are particularly important to you.

Lines of communication that are established during the pre-construction meeting must be kept open throughout the course of the project. For the owner, it can be difficult to keep up with the work at the construction site. To keep you informed, the architect will periodically assemble written summaries of the work. These summaries, called field reports are a useful tool for keeping you abreast of the progress at the job site.

Field reports

At the start of construction, the architect should begin supplying you with written field reports. These reports will be written by the architect's field representative. The field report need not be lengthy, but should cover all important information relevant to the project. Items that might be included are the progress of the work to date, notes on the acceptability of work completed, completion of the project vs. the proposed schedule and detailed information regarding particular portions of the work (i.e., structural steel, masonry, door hardware, etc.).

New and potential problems should also be identified. The timing of the field reports should parallel the pace of the work. During periods of intense activity, the architect may write bi-weekly, or even daily field reports. The clerk of the works or the building committee should review all field reports.

Change orders

Change orders are a normal, if often unwelcome, part of the construction process. With the many uncertainties inherent in a building project, it is inevitable that adjustments will have to be made en route to cope with the unexpected. They can be a source of tension within the construction team.

During construction, thousands of decisions will be made by the contractor, the architect and the owner. Many of the decisions will be made to resolve items not completely covered in the contract documents. When one of these

decisions results in a measurable change in either the contract price, the time required to complete the contract, or the scope of the final product, a change order should be prepared to formally document the changes in the construction contract.

A change order must include at least the following information:

1. The name and address of the project.
2. The number and date of the change order.
3. A written description of the change, referencing drawings and other appropriate back up material as required.
4. The change in the contract price and/or the time of the contract.
5. The new contract price.
6. The signatures of the owner, the contractor and of the architect. The signatures attest that each has reviewed the contents of the change order and agrees to the conditions of the document.

Architects commonly use Document G701, which is the standard AIA form for change orders. The standard form covers all of the above information, and is designed to be convenient and easy to understand. With change orders possessing so much potential for misunderstanding and conflict, it is important that we look the architect's and owner's roles in the change order process.

The architect's responsibilities regarding change orders

The architect is responsible for writing change orders. He or she will typically fill in all the material on the change order form, with the exception of the price, and submit the document to the contractor for pricing. The change order is then returned to the architect with the contractor's price. The architect will evaluate the price and, if no exception is taken, sign the document and forward it to the owner. If so directed, the architect should be prepared to come before the board or the building committee and explain the reasons for and the scope of, the change order.

All change orders are issued in the owner's name and are contingent upon the approval of the owner. The architect does not have the authority to approve any changes to the construction contract without the express, written approval of the owner.

The owner's responsibilities regarding change orders

The change order process represents a way for an owner to make changes to a previously signed contract without invalidating it. As they represent changes in the construction contract, change orders should come before the building committee or, preferably, before the entire board. For public agencies, the proposed changes should be reviewed and approved in an open meeting. If so directed, the architect will present a description of the proposed changes to the board along with his or her analysis of the cost of, and rationale for the changes.

If the owner requests the change order, it is the owner's responsibility to keep the work defined by the change order within the general range of the scope of work covered in the original contract. A contract for a two thousand square foot addition to a library should not be transformed by change order into a contract for a new library of 20,000 square feet. Any changes must also not be of such a nature as to render the selected contractor incapable of performing the work.

Ask the library's legal counsel if your state has any regulations controlling the extent of change orders. Some states limit the sizes of change orders in publicly-funded work to a fixed percentage of the project cost in order to insure that changes in the contract are not used as a vehicle for circumventing public bidding laws.

In addition to the potential additional cost of construction due to the change order, the owner might owe the architect additional professional fees. Architect's fees are often set as a percentage of the cost of the completed project. If this is the case, then the increase in professional fees will automatically be applied when the final cost of the project is tallied. If the architect's fee was a lump-sum arrangement based on the scope of his or her work, he or she would be justified in negotiating a increase in the professional fee to cover the additional time spent on the change order documentation.

Things can, of course, work the other way around. If a change order is required due to a mistake on the part of the architect or the con-

tractor, the cost of the change order might be borne by someone other than the owner.

Who pays?

For a two-word question, this one certainly packs a lot of punch. In our society, people seem to be more concerned with who is footing the bill than they are interested in what's being purchased. Regarding change orders, sometimes the answer to "who pays"? is straightforward, and many times it's not. The responsibility for payment of each change order must always be considered in light of the particular circumstances that resulted in the need for the change. Depending on those circumstances, the owner, the contractor, a supplier or the architect might be responsible for bearing the cost of a change order.

Although they are always issued in the name of the owner, change orders can be requested by either the owner, the contractor or the architect. Let's look at several possible scenarios that might result in the issuance of a change order, as well as at who might be responsible for footing the bill for the work.

Straightforward

During the construction project, the library director approaches the library board with a request to change the finish on the walls of his office from painted drywall to walnut paneling. "All the other library directors get walnut paneling in their offices," he says. Moved by persuasive power of his argument, the board immediately agrees to his request. You, as the chair of the building committee, direct the architect to begin a change order. In this case it's simple. The architect prepares the change order, draws a few new details and the contractor prices it. The additional cost is added to the contract and is borne by the library. Whether by a percentage fee or by negotiation, the architect's fee is increased to cover the costs of his or her time.

Not so straightforward

Your architect comes to you and reports that a basement sump pump was somehow omitted from the drawings. "Not to worry," she says, "we caught the mistake in plenty of time. Just sign this change order, and we'll have the contractor order the pump." According to the change order form, the new pump will cost

$2,000—who is going to pay for it? In a case like this, the pump should have been included in the drawings in the first place and was left off due to an error by the architect. On the other hand, it is something that you would have had to pay for anyway. In these cases, the additional cost often comes out of the money set aside for project contingency funds and the work moves on.

An hour later she comes back and reports, "I was wrong about catching the mistake in plenty of time. They poured that part of the basement slab yesterday, and we'll have to tear up some of it to install the pump. The contractor says that it's going to cost an extra $5,000 to tear up and replace the concrete." You could understand paying the $2,000 for the pump, but the additional $5,000 might be a different matter. The architect has done a lot for the library. She donated a lot of her time during the referendum, making speeches and generally helping to get your message out to the voters. What do you do? Could the additional money also come out of the project contingency or is the library required to try to get it out of the architect? What are your choices?

A fine mess...

You're spending some time working out your options, trying to figure out who is going to pay for the change order when the architect rushes in to your office. "We need a stop work order right away! I was out there watching them tear up the slab when I noticed that it was a four inch thick slab, not the six inch one shown on the drawings—the contractor should be the one paying for the replacement of the slab, not me!" Things seem to be looking up for her, and you call in the contractor to discuss the matter. The architect opens up the set of drawings, "See, here on sheet A3, the foundation detail clearly shows the slab as being six inches thick." The contractor opens up his set of drawings and flips through one dog-eared sheet after another. "Yes, but...," he begins, "The wall section details on sheets A7, A8 and A9 all show the slab as four inches thick. One place you say six inches, another place you say four inches. Which one am I supposed to believe? It looks like it's your mistake after all. And on top of that, the backhoe we brought in to tear up your slab backed into a delivery truck and smashed a load of walnut paneling. Who pays for that?"

You decide that maybe it's time to schedule a special meeting of the building committee to try to iron things out. The architect and the contractor promise to attend the meeting and, in the meantime, the project will proceed. As the Porsche and the pickup leave the parking lot, you call the personnel manager to check on how much vacation time you still have coming for the year.

I'm not going to try to untangle this one. It is just intended to illustrate how difficult it can be to stay on top of things. The general conditions of the contract usually state that the contractor is responsible for thoroughly reviewing the contract documents, noting any discrepancies and bringing them to the attention of the architect for resolution—that's why you have the pre-bid and the preconstruction meetings. But it's not necessarily that simple. Resolving situations like this will take a careful study of the contracts, as well as a close look at the relevant circumstances.

In your role as chair of the building committee, you might have been a little confused about how this matter should be settled, but you certainly did at least one thing right—you brought it to the table right away and scheduled the special board meeting to work out the issue. It can be very tempting to put matters like this aside, and delay making decisions until the end of the job when things will be a little less hectic. In practice, that's probably not a good idea. As often as not, the architect and the contractor end the project making less of a profit than they had planned during those optimistic times when the construction was just beginning. They may be in no mood to bargain when it's time for the final reckoning. In addition, closing out a project is enough of a task without adding a whole series of negotiations involving mistakes that might have been made a year or more previously. When preparing to issue a change order, always try to first settle the question of who is going to be financially responsible for it.

The seeming inevitability of changes in the work illustrate the importance of the project contingency fund. Usually around 10 percent of the estimated cost of the project, this money is held back to cover eventualities like the walnut paneling and the sump pump. When the budget begins to look tight, it's always a temptation to look at the contingency fund as a potential source of additional funding for the project. Five to ten percent should always be reserved for the unexpected.

Shop drawings

As the construction project begins, the contractor will be placing orders for many premanufactured and custom-built items that will be installed in the building. As a way of insuring that they have understood the project documents, the manufacturers will first prepare detailed drawings of items that they propose to supply to the contractor. These drawings, called shop drawings, are customarily reviewed first by the contractor, and then by the architect. Upon approval by both parties, the drawings are sent back to the manufacturer, who then fabricates the items. On occasion, the architect may consult with you regarding the acceptability of a shop drawing. For the most part however, the process is transparent to the owner—most of the review and acceptance of the drawings being undertaken by the architect and the contractor.

According to the standard AIA general conditions, the architect reviews the shop drawings only to verify that they conform with the general intent of the construction documents. The architect's approval of the drawings does not relieve the contractor of the responsibility of providing what is called for in the specifications and construction drawings. This may seem like something of a cover-your-behind move on the part of architects, but there are some sound reasons behind it. Architects are understandably reluctant to assume responsibility for someone else's drawings. As an example, some shop drawings arrive at the architect's office looking as if they had been sent over directly from NASA—impeccably drafted, dimensioned in $1/64$th of an inch increments and with copious notes to the person who will eventually fabricate the item. Other shop drawings seem like afterthoughts and look as if someone had drawn them on the back of a napkin at a truck stop. On top of it all, the quality of the shop drawings is not a certain guide to the caliber of the finished product.

The bottom line is that the sophistication of shop drawings varies greatly. Regardless of any reviews and/or approvals by the architect, the contractor is ultimately responsible for providing the owner with the building described in the contract documents.

Progress payments

The architect, as the agent of the owner, is responsible for monitoring the progress of construction and processing the contractor's pay requests. Each pay request will be evaluated by the architect before it is submitted to the owner. The architect will take a number of things into account in evaluating a request for payment. Several of the more important ones are listed below.

The schedule of values

At the beginning of the construction phase, the contractor should provide the architect and the owner with a schedule of values. The schedule of values assigns monetary values to the various general categories of the work. The work will be broken down into parts such as foundations, excavating, structural steel and masonry. The value of each portion of the work will be given. These numbers, added to the contractor's profit and overhead, will add up to the total amount of the contractor's bid.

Contractors are typically paid only for work completed as of the date of the pay request. As the schedule of values defines the worth of parts of the project, it is a valuable tool for the architect (and the owner), for comparing the contractor's requests for payment against the amount of work completed to date. Thus, if a contractor has declared that the foundation work is worth $300,000 on the schedule of values and his first pay request asks for $200,000 for foundations, it would be a relatively easy matter for the architect to verify that approximately two-thirds of the foundation work has indeed been completed.

The application for payout

The timing of the payments to the contractor was previously established in the general conditions and should have been discussed at the preconstruction meeting. As these dates draw near, the contractor will send an application for payment to the architect. This application may be in the form of standard AIA documents, or they may be the contractor's own standard forms.

Upon receipt of the application, the architect first verifies that the contractor has completed the work for which he or she is claiming payment, and then compares the amounts against the schedule of values. In addition to verifying the amount of completed work, the architect also will check that the contractor has paid his or her subcontractors and suppliers. This is an important detail as it can protect the library from legal complications.

Lien waivers

The lien waiver is the architect's prime tool for insuring that the contractor has paid any project-related debts owed to subcontractors and suppliers. The waiver itself is a preprinted form which the subcontractor or supplier fills out. The form states which project the subcontractor is working on, who he or she is working for, and how much the contractor has paid the subcontractor to date.

If a contractor retained by the library defaults on payments to subcontractors or suppliers who have provided goods and services for the construction of your project, they could file liens against your property. Often called "mechanic's liens," these instruments are attached to the title of the library's property and can prevent any transfer of the title until the payments are honored. Additionally, in many jurisdictions, they can be foreclosed like a mortgage. The threat posed to your library by liens varies from one state to another. In some states, contractors cannot file a lien against any public property. In any event, the architect will attempt to verify that the contractor has paid the subcontractors and suppliers before any payments to the contractor are approved.

Certifying the payment

After the waivers are checked and the amount of the request for payment is approved, the architect will process the pay request by issuing a certificate for payment. This completed form is forwarded to the owner, often with copies of the lien waivers. Receipt of a certified pay request indicates that the architect has evaluated the pay request and, to the best of his or her knowledge, the contractor is due the payment.

Payment

As a part of the standard AIA general conditions you, as the owner, are contractually required to make payments to the contractor in the amounts certified by the architect within a specified time frame. This protects the contractor from an owner who might wish to arbitrarily withhold a payment even if the work has been provided per the contract requirements. The general conditions also require the contractor to adhere to the architect's decisions regarding payment. If the architect determines that the contractor is due less money than he or she was asking for on the pay request, the contractor is equally bound by the architect's decision. This is another one of the occasions where the architect assumes the role of impartial arbiter of the construction contract.

Retainage

When an owner makes a payment to a contractor, a portion of the total amount due- usually in the five to ten percent range, is customarily retained by the owner until the final completion of the project. In many states, retainage is required for public work. Retainage is held by the owner to insure that the contractor will complete all the work for which he or she has contracted. At the end of each project, even after the owner has taken occupancy, there are hundreds of small items that need to be completed, adjusted or replaced by the contractor and his or her subcontractors. If the contractor has completed and been paid for 99.5 percent of the work, it might not be worth his while to send workers to the library to take care of that last half of a percent. The five or ten percent that is held back by the owner might be roughly equivalent to the contractor's profit on the project. Thus, it is a significant incentive for the contractor to fully complete the project. If a retainage is going to be withheld, the architect will account for it on the certificates for payment.

Retainage is often released to the contractor as a part of the final payment. Alternately, retainage may be partially or fully released to the contractor at some point during the project. The general and supplementary conditions to the contract will contain information regarding the disposition of the retainage. There are three items to consider if an early release of retainage is being considered. The first is that you will be giving up some of the leverage you possess to force the contractor to complete the project. Secondly, if your library is a public library, the library's attorney must verify that your state's laws permit an early release of the money. Finally, if a performance bond was required as a part of the general conditions, the contractor's bonding company must pre-approve the release of the retainage.

The punch-list

At some point the new building is declared ready to occupy. Don't confuse being ready to occupy with being complete, there will undoubtedly be many small items that will require the contractor's attention. When the building is sufficiently complete for the owner to take possession, the contractor will ask the architect to do a walk-through and record all the items that haven't been completed or that are otherwise unacceptable. This record is called the punch-list. Please refer to appendix III for an example of a punch-list. The library director or another representative of the owner should accompany the architect on the walk-though. Have the library staff prepare a list of their own and submit that list to the architect (not the contractor!) before the formal walk-through. Extra sets of eyes never hurt.

All sorts of things will appear on a punch-list— ideally none of them will be major items, as the building is supposedly ready to occupy. The entries will include things like a door frame that didn't get painted, a bad seam in the carpeting, a dripping faucet, finger marks on a ceiling tile and a squeaking belt in a rooftop ventilating unit. Don't be shy about pointing out things that do not meet with your approval. This is your chance to make sure that every detail is complete and that the taxpayers have gotten their money's worth.

A thoroughly prepared punch-list is doubly important after the building is occupied, for the contractor could rightfully claim that any defects that don't appear on the list might have been caused by the library staff or patrons, and thus are not the contractor's responsibility.

Substantial completion

When the walk-through is complete and the punchlist has been written, the architect will declare the project "substantially complete" and will issue a certificate of substantial completion. The certificate of substantial completion states that the building is sufficiently complete for the owner to occupy it for its intended use. Note that there may still be outstanding items on the punch-list at the time of substantial completion. The architect, owner and the contractor must all sign the certificate to indicate their acceptance.

The certificate of substantial completion has several important implications for you, as the owner. It is important that you understand what they are.

1. The date on which the building is declared to be "substantially complete," is the moment when the clock begins running on all the guarantees and warranties the contractor will be providing. The entire building usually is covered by a one year guarantee, while many of the items within the building may be covered with more extensive warrantees of their own. Wood doors might have a two year warranty against warping and blower motors in the air conditioning system might have a three year warranty against mechanical failure. These periods of coverage begin at substantial completion. Insofar as guarantees are concerned, it would benefit the library to delay the substantial completion for as long as possible.

2. Upon substantial completion, much of the retainage is usually returned to the contractor. If there are many items remaining on the punch-list, the library will be losing some of its bargaining power with the contractor in trying to get him or her to take care of them. You will also be losing the use of the retainage funds. In addition, punch-list items still outstanding at substantial completion will almost invariably mean headaches later. If your schedule can support a potential delay, in might be worth your while to delay the substantial completion until most of the items on the punch-list have been completed.

3. Upon substantial completion the owner assumes responsibility for providing insurance and utilities as well as building security. Any damage which occurs to the building after this date is at the owner's

expense. Have your office manager verify that the library's insurance is in order before signing a substantial completion document.

4. So far, there have been three good reasons to delay the substantial completion. On the other hand, you cannot take possession of the building until substantial completion has been declared. If you are on a tight schedule, it may even be necessary to move up the date of substantial completion and move into the building with more items on the punch-list than you would prefer. In this case, you might ask the architect if it is possible to hold on to a larger portion of the retainage to cover for the amount of work that remains.

As much of the responsibility for the building is transferred from the contractor to the owner at substantial completion, the contractor is usually anxious to have as early a date of substantial completion as possible. Knowing some of the other factors involved, you should now be better prepared to try to time this event to the best advantage of the library.

The certificate of occupancy

One of the last formalities prior to moving into your new building is obtaining the certificate of occupancy from your local building officials. Depending on where you are building, it may also be necessary to get the blessing of the state fire marshal. The local building officials have most likely been regular visitors to the construction site. They often are required to grant approvals for many of the parts of your building. Foundations, framing, electrical and plumbing systems typically are inspected as the building is being constructed. The contractor is usually responsible for calling the authorities and scheduling the inspections for the appropriate times.

If all is going well, you might not be aware of their visits. If the inspectors find some major flaw or code violations, you'll be among the first to know. Assuming that your building has passed all the interim inspections, you'll be ready to obtain the certificate of occupancy. The responsibility for obtaining this certificate, as well as others that may be required during construction is usually assigned in the general conditions of the contract. This might be a good time to review this document to satisfy yourself

that you and the other players are all fulfilling their contractual duties.

If you have a deadline for occupying the new building, it might make sense to have the architect contact the local building authorities in advance to verify that they expect to issue the certificate of occupancy in time. Nothing puts a damper on an opening day party like the building inspector unexpectedly appearing with orders to clear the building until the automatic sprinkler system has been tested and approved.

Final completion

While you were moving in and preparing to open, the contractor's crews will have been busy completing the punch-list items. Many items might still need to be addressed after you have opened the doors to the public. Eventually, the contractor will declare that all of the items on the punch-list have been completed. At this time, the contractor will send the architect a written notice of completion and request a last inspection and final payment.

According to the general conditions, the architect should promptly schedule a final walk-through to verify that all of the punch-list items have been completed to the architect's and the owner's satisfaction. A representative of the owner should again accompany the architect on the final inspection. While making the inspection, do not forget that the contractor is primarily responsible only for items that are listed on the punch-list. There are some exceptions, but the onus rests with the architect and the owner to prove that any additional unacceptable conditions did not arise since the date of substantial completion.

If the architect determines that all the outstanding items have been completed, he or she will issue a certificate of final completion to the owner. This defines the formal end of the contract time. The architect will also begin to process the contractor's final payment application. As with the other applications for payment, the architect will require the contractor to supply lien waivers from all the general contractor's subcontractors and suppliers. In this instance, all the lien waivers will be "final waivers of lien." A final waiver signifies that the general contractor has completed the contracts with his or her subcontractors and suppliers and has made final payment to them.

Before final payment can be made to the contractor, the contractor's surety company must be notified and its permission obtained. There is a standard AIA document called a consent of surety form. This form, signed by an authorized representative of the company, must be submitted by the contractor. Obtaining the surety company's approval and verifying the final waivers will help to prevent any potential challenge to the library's property. The importance of these measures cannot be overstated, especially with public property. Have the library's attorney check over and approve all the final close-out documents before signing them. When the final payment is made to the contractor, the title for the property formally passes to the owner. Under the general conditions, the contractor warrants that the property is clear of liens and other claims.

Summing up

There's a lot going on while your building is being built. Trying to keep track of who is responsible for what, and if they doing it, can be a full time job. Let's summarize some of the major duties of the principal players. I am assuming that the building is being built as a conventional design/award/build project. If it is not, some of the architect's and contractor's responsibilities may be merged.

The Owner's Responsibilities

☑ Obtain permits

The general conditions may require you to obtain building and occupancy permits. The fees for these permits are often waived for publicly owned institutions.

☑ Project financing

The owner controls and administers the contract financing. Money must be available for the payments to the contractor and the architect as they are requested. The general timing of the payments will be established at the pre-construction meeting. If the library's financing depends on property tax receipts, verify that your projected tax income will be available to the library when it is needed.

☑ Payments to the contractor

The owner is responsible for making payments to the contractor in accordance with the general conditions of the contract. The owner is contractually required to make the payments when they have been certified by the architect.

☑ Review the architect's field reports and payment certifications

Representatives of the owner must review all the material submitted by the architect.

☑ Maintain insurance

The owner must maintain insurance coverage as stipulated in the general conditions of the contract. For publicly owned institutions, there may be minimum insurance requirements. The owner will often be responsible for liability insurance and property insurance. Discuss the options with your legal counsel and insurance carrier.

☑ Attend progress and payout meetings

Representatives of the owner must attend all project meetings and should make reports to the board on a regular basis.

☑ Stopping the work

Only the owner has authority to stop the work. In the event of a major problem, the architect can only advise you to issue a stop work order. He or she cannot unilaterally issue a stop work order.

☑ Approve changes to the contract

Any changes to the contract, i.e., change orders), must be thoroughly reviewed and approved. They should be submitted by the architect in a form that is easy for the lay person to understand.

☑ Familiarity with the general conditions of the contract

The remainder of your responsibilities are spelled out in the general conditions, make sure that the building committee and the project representative are familiar with them.

The Architect's Responsibilities

The items listed below represent the minimum that you can expect from your architect on a typical project. Exact responsibilities will vary in accordance with the general conditions of the contract and the owner/architect agreement.

✔ Construction observation

The architect is responsible for periodically "observing" the construction and advising the owner of its progress and degree of conformance with the construction documents. I put "observe" in quotes because the AIA is very particular about this issue. The architect does not "inspect" or "approve" the construction; he or she only "observes" it to confirm that, to the best of his or her knowledge, the work is consistent with the contract documents.

Neither the architect nor the owner can direct the contractor to do the work in a certain manner. The final product is their primary concern, not the means of achieving it. Standard construction practice is that the "means and methods" of construction are entirely the responsibility of the contractor.

✔ Prepare field reports

The architect will prepare field reports based on what he or she has observed at the job site. These should be regularly submitted to the board. While not exhaustive, the field reports should be sufficiently detailed to record the status of the project.

✔ Process contractor pay requests

The architect must promptly process the contractor's pay requests. Both the contractor and the owner are contractually bound to abide by the architect's decisions regarding payments to the contractor.

✔ Impartially administer the construction contract

The general conditions require the architect to make impartial interpretations of the contract documents without partiality to either the contractor or the owner.

✔ Shop drawings

The architect reviews shop drawings for compliance with the contract documents. He or she will reject or modify those that are judged as being unacceptable.

✔ Clarifications of the contract documents

When inconsistencies or omissions are discovered in the contract documents, the architect issues clarifications as required. If these result in a significant change to either the scope or timing of the work, the changes will be issued in the form of change orders.

✔ Prepare change orders

The architect will prepare any change orders that may be required. He or she will analyze them and advise the owner of the fairness of the contractor's proposed costs for the additional work.

✔ Prepare the punch-list

As a final part of construction observation, the architect will prepare the punch-list to advise the owner of items not completed in accordance with the construction documents.

The Contractor's Responsibilities

Beyond the actual construction of the building, the contractor has a number of project management responsibilities. Many of them are administrative and are required by the general conditions of the contract.

✔ Provide a schedule for construction

By the time of the preconstruction meeting, the contractor should prepare and submit a proposed schedule for the project. This is important in aiding the owner in scheduling payments to the contractor

✔ Supply waivers and proof of insurance

The contractor should supply lien waivers and certificates of insurance. These are usually required in the general conditions. Have the architect, your attorney and your insurance carrier review these documents to verify that the interests of the library are being protected.

✔ As-built documents

No building is built exactly as it is drawn. Whether due to change orders or unforeseen events, there will always be some deviations to the original documents. At the close of the project, the contractor should prepare a set of record drawings documenting how the building actually went together. If the changes are small, they may be recorded as mark-ups on one of the architect's original sets of drawings. Whatever their form, these "as-built" drawings should be submitted to the owner.

Before you go...

There are a few more things that the contractor should give you before packing up. It's easy to overlook some of these details in the excitement of completing the project. Many of them are itemized in the specifications. Ask the architect to review them with you to help you determine what you should be getting. Here are some of the more common ones.

☑ Guarantees and warranties

The specifications will call for many items to have warranties beyond the standard one year general warranty for the building. Most of these will have a written warranty issued by the manufacturer or dealer. The general contractor should assemble all the specified warranties and give them to you.

☑ Additional materials

The specifications will usually require the contractor to reserve a specified percentage of certain materials and finishes used on the project and deliver them to the owner upon completion. This is especially important for items that are custom colored or are manufactured in lots that might be difficult to match at a later date. This list would include things like floor tiles, paint, wallcoverings and ceiling tiles.

☑ Keys

Check the specifications and find out how many keys that the contractor is required to supply you and see that they are properly labelled.

☑ Training

The contractor will often be required to provide library personnel with training in the operation and maintenance of systems and equipment installed as a part of his or her contract. This will include everything from the operation of sophisticated mechanical systems to cleaning instructions for vinyl flooring.

☑ Manuals

The contractor should assemble and submit the manuals with the operating and maintenance instructions for equipment installed in your new building. Manuals should be provided for heating and ventilating systems, security systems, and all other electronic and mechanical systems. Instructions for the care and maintenance for landscaping materials should also be provided.

☑ Landscape materials

A quantity of grass seed and other landscape materials should be provided to the owner. In practice, most landscape materials will be covered under the one year building guarantee so the contractor is responsible for replacing any plants that do not make it through the first seasonal cycle.

☑ Clean-up

At the close of the project, just before the owner takes occupancy, the contractor should thoroughly clean the premises, including the site. He or she should have a crew scour the building from top to bottom, cleaning up paint spatters and drywall dust, cleaning windows, picking up loose nails on the roof deck and generally making the place spotless. After the substantial completion, the library's staff will be responsible for cleaning and general maintenance of the property.

MOVING IN

And now the matchless deed's achiev'd, Determin'd, dar'd and done.
Christopher Smart

After months of construction and many, many project meetings, your building will begin to look like a library; it may even resemble the design presentation drawings that your architect showed you so long ago. If you've spent a lot of time at the job site, you have probably learned quite a bit about how a building is put together. You may have watched as the first excavations were made, as the foundations were poured and as the structural steel was erected. You may have seen masons, electricians and carpenters working side by side and wondered how they kept out of each other's way.

Thousands of parts were brought to the site and somehow assembled to make a building which beforehand, was only an abstraction on paper. The most satisfying part of it is that you have played a role in the development of that idea. Your architect may have guided the design effort, but your decisions and input are embodied in the building you see before you.

There eventually comes a day when the everything is far enough along that you can move in and begin operations. If you've ever moved into a new house, you will have some idea of what it will be like: boxes everywhere, painters and electricians hurrying to finish their work, library staff arranging furniture and moving vans shuttling back and forth.

Your new building

You probably know your building inside and out; you've made uncounted visits to the job site, and have attended the birth of your new library. Something's different now; it may suddenly strike you that this is no longer a "job site," it is your new building. Take a few moments to savor it.

Smell is the most evocative of senses. Nothing brings back distant memories better than the experience of a once familiar smell. For me, the smells of new carpeting and fresh paint with undertones of wax and furniture polish will always be linked with the excitement of moving into a new building.

Getting to know you...

New ships are taken on a shake-down cruise to work out the bugs. Your first few months in a new building will be the library's version of a shake-down cruise. You can expect to remain in regular contact with your architect and the contractor for at least a year while the building is being fine-tuned. Ventilating systems will need to be adjusted, balky door hardware fixed and minor roof leaks repaired.

The one year guarantee on your new building is intended to account for the minor items that weren't caught on the punch-list. There may be legal recourses available should a major flaw in the construction become apparent after the one year guarantee has expired. If this happens, you should discuss the matter with your architect and with the library's legal counsel. The laws protecting you in this eventuality will vary from state to state.

Stop the presses!

Even if you sponsored an event to commemorate the ground breaking, this is the time for a real celebration. Get your most creative staff members to work on ways to get the public involved in a library open house. You might consider a kid's art contest, a dog show, or a tour of the library for the media. Maybe a last section or two of sidewalk in an unobtrusive place could be poured during the festivities and local kids invited to put their handprints in it. It really doesn't matter what you do as long as it gets the public to your new library. And as before, get the newspaper people there. Cajole, bribe or threaten them until they agree to give your event the coverage that you know it deserves. With a little publicity, you should be able to instill in the community the same feeling of pride as you have in their new library.

11
Postconstruction

It ain't over till it's over. **Yogi Berra**

Readers who are parents may remember the first time that they were alone with their first child. We had our child at home. There was a nurse-midwife and a doctor in attendance. They had seen it all many times before and had quick, expert answers for nearly any question that occurred to a nervous parent. We were lucky, after the nurse and the doctor left, there were in-laws and friends there to give advice and lend support. The time came however, when the last in-law packed up to go home and friends departed to go back to their own families. After waving good-bye to the last of our helpers, we closed the front door and looked at each other. We were left with two things, a new baby and the inevitable question: "What do we do now?"

You've lived and worked in buildings your whole life. But a new building, that's a little different. Like being a first time parent, there's a lot to learn. Fortunately, there is help if you need it. When my wife and I took stock of our situation, we realized that we had two important resources at our disposal—a borrowed copy of Dr. Spock and a telephone. The professional team that helped deliver your new building will not just pack up and leave when you occupy the facility. Their expertise will still be available to you to help you work out the bugs and insure that everything in your new building works as it

was intended. When the boiler goes out on the first really cold day, or the fire alarm repeatedly goes off for no apparent reason, or the front door opens of its own volition every time the wind comes out of the north, help is as close as your telephone and that thick binder of maintenance manuals the contractor turned over to you at the close of construction.

Most postconstruction architectural services are not included in the standard owner/architect agreement. They will thus fall under the heading of "additional services." As additional services, the scope of the services and the architect's compensation for those services should be worked out in advance. In this chapter, we will look at services that you can expect the architect to provide as a part of the basic contract, and those that you might elect to add to the owner/architect agreement. I'll provide you with a "shopping list" of additional post construction services. The list can be used as a point of beginning for discussions between the board and the architect as you decide which ones might fit your situation.

What you can expect to be included

The standard AIA owner/architect contract stipulates that the architect's basic services conclude at the time of the issuance of the final certificate of payment to the contractor, or sixty days after substantial completion, whichever comes first. After that point, you could be billed for additional work on the part of the architect. The number of postconstruction services that the architect is willing to provide as a part of his or her basic agreement will depend to a large degree upon your relationship with your architect, your preferences and your in-house capabilities. Discuss these items with your architect at the beginning of the project, while you are working out the owner/architect contract to make sure that everybody has the same expectations.

As a minimum, you can expect the architect to provide the following services after you take possession of your new building.

Coordinating the final close-out

We discussed final close out services in chapter ten. I mention them here because some of them might be "postconstruction" in the sense that they can occur after you have moved into your new building. These services include everything that is required to close out the construction contract and issue the final payment to the contractor. Punch-lists, record drawings and final clean-up will be monitored to insure that the contractor has provided you with everything that was included in the contract for construction. These services are usually included under the basic agreement between you and your architect.

Correction of design flaws

Should any minor problems arise that are due to flaws in the design of your building, the architect should consult with you and provide services as required to rectify them. From the point of view of risk management, and in the interest of maintaining good client relations, the architect will usually be happy to work with you to straighten out any design related problems. Thus, if two doors interfere with each other when both are open, or if there is an area of the reading room with an unacceptably low level of illumination, the architect should coordinate any modifications required to make things right.

Because of the growing complexity of modern buildings, it is not unusual for problems to crop up in the mechanical and electrical systems. Systems that were previously simple, stand-alone arrangements are increasingly linked electronically to enhance building safety and energy efficiency. The architect and his or her consultants are frequently called in to adjust or modify building systems to get them running within specifications.

We will look at some other aspects of problems related to faulty design later in this chapter. In the meantime, let's consider an important facet of postconstruction services.

You get what you pay for

This will be a significant theme when we discuss the selection of architects. I said that many postconstruction services are not explicitly included in the standard owner/architect contract and that the number of "additional" services that you receive without additional fees depends on your relationship with your architect. If you selected your architect primarily by price shopping, it stands to reason that the lower-priced architects might have been able to offer that lower rate by cutting back somewhere. Postconstruction services are frequently the first things that will be scaled back by an architect looking to reduce the professional fee. If you are comparing the proposed services of several architects, be sure that they are planning to include similar scopes of post construction assistance.

Before beginning a project, it is difficult to estimate what the value of the architect's postconstruction services will be to you. If everything goes smoothly and you have a good contractor, few services may be required after you take occupancy of the building. If the picture isn't so rosy, you and the architect might be seeing a lot of each other. This may result in some significant and unexpected bills unless compensation was agreed upon beforehand.

Optional postconstruction services

Here are some other commonly offered postconstruction services. As "additional services," the prices for each should negotiated as a part of the owner/architect contract. There is space at the end of the standard AIA contract for identifying the scope and cost of additional services. Some of these services are typically provided shortly after taking occupancy of the building while others imply a long-term relationship between the architect and the client.

✔ Furniture arrangement and selection

For a single person office, it's not usually too challenging to find a satisfactory furniture arrangement. Identifying an efficient arrangement for large areas combining stacks, reference desks, reading tables and clerical space is more difficult. The architect can generate detailed plans to help you identify the most efficient use of your space. In addition, he or she can generate lists of your furniture requirements to aid you in ordering new furnishings and can also provide you with estimated costs. The costs of furnishing a new building are often overlooked. Having a furniture plan will be an important part in determining the final cost of your project.

✔ Interior design services

Beyond developing a furniture plan, architects can often provide interior design services, providing assistance with the selection of furniture, wall coverings, carpeting, window treatments, etc. If you wish, the architect could also work with an interior designer of your choice. Keep in mind that if you plan to use some of your existing furniture, new purchases will have to be coordinated with it. Furniture and other interior finishes are expensive, and they may have to be let out for competitive bids. If so, the architect can write the specifications and coordinate the bidding.

✔ Mechanical and electrical changes

After you've been in your building for a some time, you may identify changes that you would like made to the mechanical and electrical systems. Maybe a new computer generates more heat than was anticipated, additional security lighting is required around the building or more outlets need to be installed to accommodate new equipment. If the change is simple, like a few additional electrical outlets, you could hire a local electrician to make the changes. For additional site lighting, or major adjustments to a cooling system, it might be appropriate to retain the architect to coordinate the work and insure that you are getting the most for your money.

✔ Scheduling the move

Complicated moves can require some intensive scheduling and logistical work to bring every-thing off smoothly. With his or her detailed knowledge of the building schedule and of how you operate, the architect is well placed to aid you in coordinating your move. The architect can work with the moving company to design an efficient strategy for the move that will minimize both your down-time and your aggravation. The more critical your schedule, the more you should consider retaining the architect to assist in coordinating the move.

✔ Coordinating and checking the record drawings

There is considerable variation in the quality of the as-built drawings as prepared by building contractors. After your building is finished, an accurate set of as-built drawings will be an invaluable resource.

An example...

I once was the structural engineer for a project in a large city in which the owners of a disused 1920s era department store building asked us to determine if it could be transformed from a department store into (believe it or not) a multi-story parking garage. None of the original drawings could be located, so we set to the task of determining the structural capacity of the old building. The building's frame was made of concrete. In order to determine its strength, we were going to have to literally jackhammer portions of it apart to determine the sizes and spacing of the steel reinforcing bars within.

We began by measuring the building. One day, after about a week of work in the cold and echoing interior, I was measuring the elevator penthouse and discovered a complete set of as-built drawings where they had fallen behind an old desk. That discovery saved us weeks of work, and the owners tens-of-thousands of dollars.

This is admittedly an extreme example. The chances of you wanting to convert your library into a parking garage are probably pretty slim. There is, however, a fairly good possibility that an addition or substantial remodeling will be done at some point in the future. An accurate set of as-built drawings is an insurance policy against unpleasant and potentially expensive surprises. A commonly encountered problem is uncertainty about the true sizes and locations of existing footings and other underground structures. This is particularly a concern when trying to add an addition to an existing building where the discovery of an unanticipated footing or underground utility can be a serious setback. Other kinds of as-built information that can be useful at a later date are the color selections and the names of the manufactures for finish materials such as wallpaper, paint and carpeting, bricks and door hardware.

It is particularly important that the as-built drawings reflect design changes due to change orders and other modifications made during construction as they will not appear on the original construction documents. If you wish, the architect can check and assemble the record documents to insure that the information that the contractor provides you is accurate, complete and usable. Lastly, record documents must be updated from time to time over the life of the building to record the inevitable changes that are made. Even though the architect may not be involved with each project, he or she can continue to update the drawings on a regular basis to keep them current. In the age of computer aided drafting, this task is becoming easier than ever. In previous times, as-built architectural documents became palimpsests of erasures and redrawing. Rather than relying an old, yellowed piece of tracing paper bearing the marks of years of modifications, the computerized architect makes the required changes to a file on a floppy disk and has the computer print out a new drawing sheet which replaces the old.

✔ The ten-month building inspection and warranty review

When the substantial completion paperwork is signed, the clock begins ticking on the warranties and guarantees that cover your building. Many of those warranties expire after one year, including the whole building warranty provided by the general contractor. I recommend that you consider hiring the architect to make a thorough inspection of the building ten months after substantial completion. In ten months, your building will have undergone a nearly complete seasonal cycle and many of the problems that occur due to thermal expansion and contraction will have become apparent. After a thorough inspection of the structure, the architect should put together what is essentially a punch-list of items that must be fixed by the contractor under the terms of the whole building warranty. The architect can then observe the

work to verify that it is done according to the contract. As during the construction period, the architect should issue field reports to the board to keep them informed of the progress of the work.

While the contractor is busy with any work covered under the whole building warranty, the architect can assemble all the other component warranties that come with your building and have each item checked out to verify that it is functioning as intended. Equipment manufacturers or their local suppliers will often come to the site to do a warranty inspection. Sometimes it is automatic, and sometimes you have to ask for the inspection. The architect can coordinate this process to help you identify and get any services that you are due.

✔ Long-term planning

After you move into your new library, you will undoubtedly discover things that you will wish that you had done differently. Some of them can be addressed by adapting your procedures, while others might call for changes in the building plan or equipment. The library director should always have a long-term capital improvement plan to accommodate the changing needs and situation of the library. Some new requirements may come from outside the library, as is illustrated by the Americans With Disabilities Act. This is an example of federal legislation that can require existing libraries to make changes to their facilities. In this case, the purpose of the changes is to make all public facilities uniformly accessible to the handicapped. The architect can assist the library director in identifying potential projects and in analyzing their feasibility. This process resembles the programming phase that began your project. Using interviews and other data-gathering techniques, the architect will assist you in identifying your present and future needs and in setting appropriate goals.

Your architect can suggest additional postconstruction services that he or she feels are particularly suited to your needs. Many of these services do not need to be determined when the contract is signed with the architect, they can be provided later, on an as-needed basis. The provider can be the original architect for your building, or another if there was some dissatisfaction with the original arrangement. That brings us to another important "record document" that can be of some use to you as well as other libraries in your area.

EVALUATING THE PROJECT

After the project is completed and all the contracts are closed out, you may wish to assemble the staff and the board members who were involved and sit them down for a debriefing session. At a debriefing, you can discuss the successes, the mistakes and lessons that were learned during the long process of planning and constructing a new building. This would be the time to try to frame as objective an evaluation as possible of your architect and of the relative success of your project.

The "success" of a project can be difficult to determine. No building is everything that you wish it could be. A thousand small, and sometimes not so small, compromises have to be made to make a building a reality in the light of monetary realities, site restrictions and conflicting program requirements. The more that you were involved in the process, the greater will be your understanding of the decisions that had to be made en route.

The building

There are a few objective evaluations that you can make of the tangible product of your enterprise. Many comments will, by their nature, be more subjective. The evaluations can be discussed and the conclusions noted. A scorecard could also be developed to aid in your evaluation. Here are some of the questions that should be considered.

1. *Was the building completed on time?*

2. *Was the cost of the building within the stated budget, including contingencies?*

3. *Were substantial change orders required? "Substantial" in this case might be defined as anything over seven percent or so of the anticipated cost of the project for a new building. For an addition or remodeling the percentage of the change orders might be higher.*

4. *Were all the original program requirements met?*

5. *As the 1940s big band leader Ted Lewis used to say, "Is everybody happy?" You couldn't ask a more subjective question. It*

is, however, guaranteed to spur some discussion.

6. *Do the patrons like it? If there are some criticisms, make a note of them for discussion with the architect.*

7. *Were the design goals met, and did they prove to be appropriate?*

8. *Is the building what you were expecting, or were you surprised at the end product?*

The architect

The architect can be evaluated both in terms of the perceived success of the project, and in terms of the service that he or she provided. Some of the questions will necessarily overlap with the ones given above.

1. *Did the architect provide all the services that were specified in the contract?*

2. *During the programming phase, was the data efficiently collected and were the program requirements satisfied in the end product?*

3. *Did the architect make appropriate use of materials provided by the library building consultant (if any)?*

4. *Was the architect responsive when you had questions or needed clarifications?*

5. *Was the architect willing to modify the design when requested to do so by the board?*

6. *Was the building produced on budget and in time?*

7. *Did change orders during construction increase the cost of the building more than seven percent beyond the initial bid amount?*

8. *If the answer to either of the above questions was "no," was it due to poor service on the part of the architect?*

9. *Did the architect provide a leadership role in the design and building process?*

10. *Were the architect's budget estimates realistic?*

11. *Were the architect's estimates of the time required for construction realistic?*

12. *Did the architect adequately represent the library in negotiations with civil and municipal authorities?*

13. *Did the architect adequately represent the library in dealings with the contractor?*

14. *Was the architect easy to work with? Did he or she give due attention to your needs?*

15. *Was the total of the professional fees paid to the architect consistent with what you were led to expect?*

16. *Do you feel that you received good value for the money that you spent for professional services?*

17. *Is the building, considering necessary compromises, what you wanted?*

18. *Would you use this architect again?*

The questions on this list may sound something like those that you would ask while selecting an architect. Many of them are, and we shall make use of this material when we discuss how to hire an architect in chapter twelve.

Many library systems and state libraries maintain lists and evaluations of library consultants for the use of the member libraries. Send a copy of your evaluations to them so other libraries can benefit from your experiences. Some of them may already have standard questionnaires for you to use to help you in evaluating professional consultants.

The library organization

The ultimate success of your project depended, to a large degree, on the library staff and board of directors. There are a few questions that you should ask yourselves to help evaluate your own performance.

1. *Did the in-house chain of command work effectively and efficiently?*

2. *If the answer to the above question is "no," what would you do differently next time?*

3. *Did you respond promptly when the architect had questions or needed clarifications?*

4. *Were disagreements within the in-house project team effectively resolved?*

5. *Was the information provided by the library building consultant useful in the programming of the building?*

6. *Was the original financial planning done by the library staff and consultants valid?*

7. *Was the library prompt in obtaining insurance and permits as required by the contract?*

8. *Were requests for payment by the contractor promptly honored?*

9. *Does the library have the in-house expertise to maintain and operate the mechanical and electrical systems in the new building?*

10. *Did the staff and members of the building committee give the project the time it deserved?*

A debriefing is one way of summarizing the project and of putting the construction phase behind you. It marks the end of what may have been a two or three year journey. If the project went smoothly, the final punch-list and close-out probably also went well. There are times, however, when those last few items on the punch-list seem never to be completed, or when defects start showing up right after you occupy the building. In those cases, things can drag on for quite a while you are waiting for the problems to be fixed. That last payment to the contractor, the one that isn't made until the items on the punch-list are completed, is usually enough of an incentive to guarantee that the work will be completed. What happens when problems aren't apparent until after the contractor has cashed the final check? Or if you think that they may be due to faulty design on the part of the architect?

Pointing fingers

Discussing the subject of potential problems in the design of a building makes me acutely aware that I am wearing (at least) two hats here. As an architect, I want to say "Take it easy on the designer; everybody makes mistakes." As a library trustee, I want to advise you to try to find satisfaction wherever you can to insure that the taxpayers are getting their money's worth. One hat that I'm definitely not wearing is that of an attorney. Whenever there is a question of payment for damages, the library should discuss the matter with its legal counsel. Every problem has to be examined in its own light. Unfortunately, it's easier to point a finger than to solve a problem, and finger pointing often begins before the problem is even defined.

Identifying the problem is the first, and perhaps the most important task. There are so many possibilities that I can't hope to give enough examples to be a useful guide to solving your own construction-related problems. The best we can do here is to offer some advice that might help you define a problem. Once a problem is defined, a solution often suggests itself.

Postconstruction problems can be grouped into three rough categories—problems related to faulty design, those related to defective construction, and those caused by improper use. This grouping implies a distinct division of responsibility for a particular problem. In reality, things are seldom so clear cut. We will first take a look at problems that might be attributed to an error on the part of the architect.

Design flaws — continued

The assessment of responsibility for shortcomings in the design of the building can be difficult. This gets back to the uncomfortable question of "who pays" that was posed when we were discussing change orders. There are two general kinds of design flaws. The first kind of flaw is one that compromises part of the building program and makes the building less useful to you. The second kind would be something that might result in an unsafe condition and contribute to the chances of an accident or injury.

Book im-mobile

The first kind of design problem might be illustrated by the following example. Say that your library is substantially complete and you're beginning to move in. The library driver delivers the bookmobile from its former home at the old building to the new garage. Just before he pulls the vehicle in, someone notices that the top of the bookmobile is several inches higher than the underside of the garage door.

You could argue that the designer should have been aware of the size of the vehicle and might have a case for a claim against the architect for the cost of the required modifications to the garage. If, on the other hand, the bookmobile was purchased new and turns out to be too large for the door opening, you would be faced with some different questions. First, was the architect aware that the garage was intended to house a bookmobile? If so, did the library make the measurements available to the architect in time to incorporate them into the design? Maybe the library staff did not know the dimensions of the bookmobile when the building was being designed. You still might ask if the door height is sufficient to clear the "typi-

cal" bookmobile. If it could be demonstrated that the door is large enough for the average bookmobile, and that the library had purchased one that was unusually tall, the architect could say that the difficulty arose due to the library's failure to supply the designer with needed information.

The best thing that you, as the owner, can do to avoid bearing the responsibility for this kind of dilemma is to be sure that your needs are effectively expressed to the architect during the programming and design phases of the project. The success of this will depend largely on how well your in-house team is organized and managed. A good architect should identify most of the building requirements by asking questions during the programming phase. That does not, however, relieve the owner of the responsibility of identifying special items that the architect might miss, and of transmitting the information to the architect. Another thing to remember is that the library board signed off on the plans during the design phase. An architect cannot realistically expect laypeople to go over a set of building plans with a fine tooth comb and identify every potential shortcoming, but this does illustrate the importance of the milestone reviews and of the owner's responsibility for thoroughly examining the drawings before approving them.

The second type of design flaw is the kind that might result in an accident or an injury. It is always a cause for concern, and perhaps a reason for immediate action. The aim of the architect is to give you the building that you want. Whatever your requirements, it is the duty of the architect to design the building in such a way that it promotes the health, safety and welfare of the public. You rely on the architect's professional expertise to produce a safe building while fulfilling the objectives expressed in the building program. There is also the additional safety net comprised by the building codes, which typically set the minimum standards of safety for your building. You assume that the architect is familiar with the applicable codes and that your building will conform with them.

Many potentially serious design flaws are not covered by building codes. This is where you have to depend on the architect's experience and common sense.

An example of a potentially dangerous flaw might be something as simple as some improper grading adjacent to a sidewalk which causes water to run over the walk during a rain. By itself, this condition is not particularly dangerous. Combine it with freezing temperatures, however, and you have a situation where someone could fall and be injured. If the grading was done as it was drawn on the construction documents, the architect might bear some responsibility in case of an accident.

The degree of the architect's responsibility for fixing design flaws depends on several things. First, the design of the item in question must have been included in the architect's contract. If the owner had a direct contract with a security company to install a burglar alarm system for the new building, the architect bears no responsibility if the system fails to function as advertised. Secondly, the problem must not have arisen due to faulty maintenance on the part of the library. This is especially important when it comes to complex mechanical systems. Finally, whatever is causing you problems must be used as it would be reasonably inferred by the architect. If the library staff suspends a heavy display from the suspended ceiling grid and the grid sags, the architect would have no responsibility for the condition unless he or she was instructed by the client that the grid should be designed to support the additional load.

Before laying blame for what is assumed to be a design problem, schedule a meeting with the architect to discuss the matter. What may, at first, seem to be a design omission might later prove to be the result of a miscommunication within the project team. In the event that someone claims that a design error causes an injury, or in cases of disasters like structural failures, many states will allow the library to take legal action against the architect at least until the expiration of the statute of limitations. As always, the library's lawyer should be consulted.

Construction flaws

Everybody has heard of construction failures. Most of them are not dramatic. The lineup is comprised mostly of things like leaky roofs, cracked foundation walls, doors that don't close and windows that won't open. On occasion, the television news will show pictures of a building that suffered a catastrophic collapse. Such failures are rare in the United States due to the enforcement of building codes and the overall quality of construction here.

A leaky roof, or a cracked foundation wall on your building will probably not make the six o'clock news, but it is important to you. The real question is what to do about it. Whatever the problem, the first thing to do is to try to identify its cause and determine if it is covered under a warranty. If there is warranty coverage, you can contact the contractor and schedule the required repairs. Remember that the entire building is typically covered under a one year warranty, while some components like roofs and mechanical equipment may be covered for longer periods.

If the problem occurs after the expiration of the one year building warranty, and is not covered by an individual warranty, you may have several options. We're going to assume that the problem is, in fact, due to faulty construction and not due to something reaching the end of its anticipated life span, or the result of poor maintenance. First, call the contractor and tell him or her of the situation. If the contracting company has an ongoing relationship with the library, they may come out and make the fix at their own cost in the interest of maintaining good relations with a valued client. If the contractor claims that your problem is not the result of faulty construction, or refuses to make repairs without charging the library, you may have to turn to the architect to assist you in demonstrating that the work did not meet the specifications.

Showing that part of a building was not built according to the construction documents can be difficult. Sometimes the procedure is invasive in the sense that portions of the building might have to be removed to gain access to the component in question. It might be as easy as lifting up some ceiling tiles to expose a steel beam to verify that the correct size beam was installed. If your concrete foundation wall is cracking, it is a relatively simple matter to have the concrete tested to verify that its strength is up to specifications. If you are questioning whether or not the contractor put the proper amount of reinforcing steel inside the concrete wall, it will require a more thorough (and hence, more expensive) investigation.

If you wind up in the situation of having to verify beam sizes to check up on a contractor's work, you might find yourself questioning the value of the architect's job site observations. It is worth repeating that the purpose of the architect's field observations is not to ferret out every construction flaw, but rather to confirm general compliance with the contract documents. There are so many things going on simultaneously at a construction site that it is virtually impossible to guarantee that everything has been built exactly according to the plans. Engaging a full-time field representative will not eliminate problems with poor construction, but it can help to reduce the chances of a serious shortcoming.

Gentlemen, start your lawyers!

There is always the potential that there will be a disagreement between the contractor and the architect in establishing the liability for poor construction. Not surprisingly, this often takes the form of each insisting that the other is responsible. The architect may maintain that the problem is due to faulty construction on the part of the contractor, and the contractor may declare that it is the result of poorly drawn or detailed architectural documents. If no agreement can be reached, expert third party opinions might have to be obtained and the matter settled in the courts. Get the library's attorney involved if you are in the position of having to demonstrate poor workmanship on the part of a contractor. The rules for documenting your investigations can be very specific and will vary from state to state. Depending on the laws in your state, your protection against faulty construction could extend up to, and perhaps beyond the statute of limitations.

Back to the beginning

We have come a long way in the last eleven chapters. We began by discussing the need for the client to understand the architect's vocabulary and then looked at each part of a "typical" architectural project. You've learned what happens during each phase of the undertaking. At this point, you have an overview of the kinds of services that architects provide, and at least a general idea of what you can expect them to do for you.

There is another important part of the process that we should look at, one that occurs before your project is begun. In the next chapter, we will not be discussing architectural services themselves, but rather who is going to provide those services and how you should go about finding and selecting your architect.

12
Finding, Selecting and Hiring an Architect

The winds and the waves are always on the side of the ablest navigators.
Edward Gibbon

I find the great thing in this world is not so much where we stand, as in what direction we are moving.... **Oliver Wendell Holmes**

Choosing your navigator

It was July 2, 1937, and the US Coast Guard Cutter Itasca was anchored off Howland Island, the northernmost island of the Phoenix Island group in the South Pacific. The Itasca and her crew were waiting for Amelia Earhart. Amelia and her navigator, Fred Noonan, were on one of the last legs of a record-breaking trip around the world. They were flying over the Pacific and they were lost.

In his prime, Noonan had been one of the best navigators around. He had been one of the chief navigators for Pan American when the airline established its "China Clipper" service across the Pacific. He was also an alcoholic and the years of drinking had taken their toll. By the time of Amelia's around the world attempt he was, perhaps, no longer the right man for the job. Seeing this, many of her friends had advised her against using him.

At Howland Island the radiomen aboard the Itasca could hear Amelia as she tried to contact them. Because of inappropriate radio equipment aboard the plane and a lack of coordination between her and the Coast Guard, she could not hear their replies. "We are circling but cannot hear you..." she called. According to Noonan's calculations they should have been right over Howland but there was nothing below but ocean. Over and over, Amelia called the Itasca. The radiomen could hear the frustration in her voice as her fuel supply ran low. Eventually, her transmissions ceased. An extensive search failed to come up with any trace of the aircraft.

Amelia has always been one of my heroines, although my estimation of her was slightly diminished when I learned that poor planning had played such a major role in her disappearance.

Navigation is a tricky thing. Over a long trip, the consequences of even a small error can grow until you are far from your intended position. It takes knowledge and care to do it right. An architect has much in common with a navigator. In each project, the architect is presented with a destination and is expected to find the path of least resistance to attain it. Based on our research and experience, we may even advise that the ultimate goal be reconsidered. In the end, however, it is the client who decides. Selecting the right navigator is an important part of planning your journey. In this chapter, I'll give you a method for finding and selecting an architect, along with suggestions on negotiating fees and contracts. As with all journeys, good preparation is everything.

Without a clue

We recently had a request for proposal arrive in our office. As they represent potential work, requests for proposal are always welcome and we respond to them immediately. This proposal was from a nearby municipality. They wished to build several new buildings in an existing park as well as develop the site by providing new electrical service, sewers and a well.

There were brief descriptions of each building and a list of architectural services that were to be included. The list contained many of the services that we have been looking at in the preceding chapters. Here's what they were seeking:

1. Programming to identify space requirements.
2. Preparation of alternative designs and budgets.
3. Final design and budget.
4. Permit applications.
5. Construction observation.

The request for proposal asked us to submit our qualifications, resumes of key personnel and professional fees, with the fees broken down for each phase of the work.

The first alarm bells went off when we got to the part requesting fees. While the work was outlined in broad terms, the brief descriptions of the buildings weren't enough for us to begin estimating the time it would take us to design and draw them. In addition, there were no clues that we could use to evaluate the magnitude of the civil engineering work that it would take to supply the site with water, sewer and electricity. Were existing sewers and waterlines close by and easy to connect to, or were they located a half mile away on the other side of a federally-protected wetland?

The request for fees presented another problem. In many states, including ours, most public bodies are legally prohibited from requesting professional fees from architects in a request for proposal. We'll look at this later when we discuss qualifications-based selection. Our dilemma was twofold. Should we inform the municipality that they were violating the law and possibly get the reputation of being a "squeaky wheel," and thus potentially lose our chance of being selected, or should we ignore the regulation and proceed with our response in the hope that we would be the low bidder? The second choice came with the added potential that someone could legally challenge our contract with the city as being illegal and have us pulled off the job, possibly without being compensated for services that we may have provided. We decided to proceed cautiously until we could evaluate the situation.

Flying blind

When we called the contact person at the city with our questions about the size of the project, we found that he didn't have any estimates of the proposed budget or eventual square footage of the buildings. Furthermore, no one had any information regarding existing utilities or of the potential problems in getting them to the project site. We were now in the position of having to put a lot of up-front time into evaluating the feasibility of the project and the site conditions in order to come up with a realistic fee.

Our dilemma was finally resolved when we got our contact at the city to admit that the city fathers were planning to spend "around $150,000" on the project. We realized that with all the unknowns, we might easily spend the potential fee for a project this size in doing the up-front work required to put together our proposal. It looked like a lose-lose situation. If we weren't selected, we would be in the red for the substantial amount of money we spent trying to define their project. If we were selected, the fee would probably be barely enough to recoup our up-front expenses, not to mention paying us for the programming, design work and construction documents.

We decided to write the city a letter thanking them for their interest in us but declining to submit a proposal.

This story might remind you of the reroofing project we looked at back in chapter three. You have to know which questions to ask and what information to give if you want to get a quality product. Defining your needs and identifying your goals are the first steps.

THE PROCESS

The process of hiring an architect can be broken into seven basic steps. For public institutions, some of the details will differ from one state to another. Always ask your lawyer to inform you of any local requirements. Before you even consider construction you will have to debate one of the first points raised in this book, namely, "Is this trip really necessary?" If you are convinced that it is, read on.

STEP 1.   EVALUATE THE NEED FOR AN ARCHITECT

If your project is a building or an addition, you will probably be legally required to hire a licensed architect. For smaller projects, it will often be something of a judgment call. Weigh your in-house resources against the task. If you want to put up some knee walls to subdivide an area in the children's library and your building engineer is good at carpentry, you can probably skip hiring an architect. Even this example is not as simple as it sounds. The smallest of projects can still raise questions regarding required paths of egress for fire exiting and regulations regarding the use of combustible materials in construction. If you're considering reroofing or spending $50,000 on new carpeting, I would strongly advise you to hire an architect to write specifications and to oversee the bidding process. One additional test that you could apply involves the need for a building permit. If the project you are planning requires a permit, there is a good chance that drawings or calculations will have to be produced by a licensed architect or engineer.

Consider the professional fees on smaller projects to be "expert insurance" that can provide a better finished product and also help to insulate the library from potential liability. On some occasions, it is appropriate to hire engineering consultants directly without first hiring an architect. An example of this might be renovations to a boiler or plumbing system, for this kind of work it would be appropriate to hire a local mechanical/plumbing engineering firm.

STEP 2.   DETERMINE THE SCOPE OF SERVICES THAT YOU NEED.

A thorough examination of your goals is the first stage in determining the services that you will want an architect to provide. A defined list of services will help to insure that the same standards are used in your evaluation of each of the potential architects as well as aid you in the preparation of a request for proposal.

You will have a head start if you are utilizing the services of a library building consultant. The document produced by the building consultant will set your initial course as the consultant's research will identify many of your initial requirements. With the consultant's report in hand, there are a number of general questions that you should consider.

A. *What is lacking in your current facility?*

B. *Is expansion of your services a goal?*

C. *Is expansion of the size of your present facility a goal?*

D. *Which parts of your facility and what aspects of your services need to expand?*

E. *If you are contemplating an addition, which services will be housed in the new space?*

F. *Are there any time constraints associated with your potential project? An example of this would be the planned demolition of the existing library due to municipal plans to widen a road or develop a new scheme for the city center. If there are timing requirements, plot them out; this will form the basis for a project time line.*

G. *At this time, do you intend to only test the waters with a feasibility study and an estimated cost for the work, or do you have to commit to design and build a new building?*

H. *Do you have to pass a referendum to accomplish your building goals?*

I. *Do you want continuous input into the design process, or will "milestone" reviews be sufficient?*

Once these questions have been considered, you are ready to begin defining the scope of services that you will itemize in your request for proposal

No building consultant?

If you are not using a library building consultant, you may wish to consider hiring an architect on a preliminary basis to prepare a building program. The services that a library building consultant provides overlap to a large degree with those that an architect would provide in assembling a building program. A library building consultant is an expert at programming libraries; he or she will probably provide you with more detailed information than would an architect. Depending on where you are located, however, a library building consultant may not be required or even be available.

Programming is not a part of the basic services in a standard architectural contract. As an additional service, it is often negotiated as a separate line item and thus is a relatively easy item to break out as a distinct contract. You could use this program in lieu of a library building consultant's report while evaluating what services you need and while preparing your request for proposal. If this method is chosen, the architect could be retained on the understanding that the current relationship ends with the end of the building programming and that he or she would be among the group of architects considered at a later date for the remainder of the work. As an alternate possibility, there are individuals who bill themselves as building programmers rather than architects. If there are any of them in your area, they would be able to provide the same service.

In choosing a consultant to provide a building program, you could use an simplified version of the method for selecting an architect that will be presented in this chapter. Previous experience in programming similar size institutions and good references will be of primary importance.

There are several advantages in having a building program in hand when you begin your search for the architect who will design your building. One is that a potential architect will have a good idea of the size of the project and will be able to fine tune the scope and the price of his or her proposed services. If you eliminate some of the uncertainties, the architect will not have to arbitrarily increase the fee to cover the unknowns, thus resulting in cost savings for the library. The other major advantage is that a building program is a large component of a feasibility study. Once you know the approximate size of the possible project, it is a relatively easy matter to use some local cost per square foot figures for other buildings and get a rough idea of its potential cost.

THE MENU
Let's review the services that you might need for a typical project. Though this book is primarily aimed at libraries, this information will apply to almost any building type.

Pre-Design (Additional) Services
Programming
Programming will be required to accurately identify your needs. Based on the material above, this can be done by either a library building consultant, an architect, or a professional programmer. Programming may be done before the consultant for the remainder of the architectural project is selected. Note that if the initial program is done by a library building consultant, additional architectural programming will be required to cover items not included in the library consultant's report.

Site Analysis
Site analysis is required for almost any project that involves new construction. An analysis may be performed for several different sites to aid in the determination of which one to purchase. Like programming, it is not part of the basic services and is often negotiated separately. Site analysis and programming are termed "predesign" services. Some architects may elect to include site analysis as a part of their basic services if you know which site you are going to use for your building. If part of the scope of work involves site selection, you will probably have to pay for additional services.

Feasibility Study
If you need general information about the potential for building a new library or an addition, you can commission an architect to perform a feasibility study. Site analysis and programming are often included as parts of a feasibility study. A three-part study consisting of programming, site analysis and a building feasibility study should be sufficient to give you a general indication of the viability of your potential project.

Referendum Assistance
If a referendum is required to fund your project, you may wish to have the architect assist you by preparing visual displays and other materials that will get your message out to the public. If the architect has a talent for public speaking, you might also be able to use those skills to your advantage. If an architect has been

awarded a project that depends upon a referendum, he or she will often be willing to donate some time to help you get your issue approved by the voters. If you want the architect to prepare renderings of what your building may look like, you may have to authorize the him or her to continue into the schematic design phase.

Contract Basics

Schematic Design

Schematic design is included in a standard AIA owner/architect contract as one of the basic services. It is an essential part of the process of designing a new building. The general layout and appearance of the building are defined during this time. If information about the building characteristics is important to your referendum effort, you may wish to have the architect complete the schematic design before launching your publicity drive. Schematic design can also be included as a part of a thorough feasibility study. A schematic design enables the architect to generate a more accurate estimate of the probable construction cost of the building. If schematic design is included as a part of a feasibility study, the remainder of the architect's basic services could be made contingent upon the passage of the referendum or the availability of funding.

Schematic design comprises approximately 15% of the architects basic services fee.

Design Development

The schematic design for your project is refined and developed into a complete building design during design development. At this stage, the architect will retain and coordinate the work of a number of different consultants. Design development is usually not undertaken until funding for the project is secured.

Design development comprises approximately 20% of the architects basic services fee.

Construction Documents

Construction documents is the most time-consuming portion of an architect's contract. Construction documents are expensive and are not generally done unless project funding is assured. If project funding will not be available in the near future, you can consider delaying the construction documents phase until the time of construction is closer at hand. This will insure that code changes that may have taken effect in the interim are accounted for on the drawings.

Construction documents comprise approximately 40% of the architects basic services fee.

Bidding

The architect will provide assistance throughout the bidding process; preparing bid forms, procuring bids, and answering contractor's questions. The analysis and evaluation of bids is also a critical step in awarding a contract. The architect or engineer who prepared the drawings should evaluate the bids and report to the board.

Bidding comprises approximately 5% of the architects basic services fee.

Construction Administration

While it is a part of the basic services, there are a number of options open to you regarding the administration of the construction contract. The most common ones are as follows;

1. *Construction administration by the architect.*

For most projects, it makes sense to have the architect, as the person most intimately familiar with the building, over see the administration of the construction contract. Construction administration represents approximately twenty percent of an architect's contract in a standard arrangement. If you wish full-time representation on the site, you will usually have to pay the architect additional professional fees.

2. *Construction administration by a construction manager.*

For very large or complex projects, you can retain a construction manager to oversee the work. This is often done as an alternative to full time field observation by the architect. If you choose to hire a construction manager, you will still need to retain the architect to provide some services during the construction phase to offer clarifications and make any required adjustments to the construction documents.

3. *In-house construction administration.*

You can have your staff handle the construction administration if you have personnel with the required expertise. In this case, you may still wish to hire the architect for clarifications and adjustments. Be advised that construction administration can be very time-consuming and requires a thorough knowledge of construction practices.

Construction administration comprises approximately 20% of the architects basic services fee.

Postconstruction Services

Postconstruction services are additional architectural services that can extend the architect's quality control beyond the close of the construction contract. Most post construction services are not included in the standard owner/architect contract. As additional services, they are negotiated separately. Examples of common postconstruction activities by the architect were listed in chapter eleven. These services do not need to be itemized when you negotiate the original contract with the architect. Rather than commit to a full range of post construction services early on, you can opt to have the architect provide the services on a as-needed basis, perhaps on an hourly rate arrangement. If you choose this option, have the architect submit a listing of the hourly rate(s) that would be used when and if you require post construction services. You should not expect to pay the architect for postconstruction services that are clearly required because of a mistake or oversight on the part of the architect.

STEP 3.   WRITING THE REQUEST FOR PROPOSAL

Even if you are sure which architects that you will be interviewing for your project, you should write a request for proposal (RFP). It is an important tool which helps to standardize the procedures that you are going to use to interview and hire an architect. After the board has agreed upon the scope of services that is going to be required for the project, the preparation of the RFP can begin.

Please refer to appendix I for a sample request for proposal. In putting it together, I gleaned what I felt were the best parts of a number of actual requests for proposal that came to our office. This format is just a suggestion. All that matters is that you cover the important information in a clear and easy to understand manner.

A question of money

There is always a question as to whether or not you should request fees as part of an architectural proposal. I have some strong feelings on the matter, as you'll discover shortly. For the moment, we'll ignore the possibility that depending upon where you live, it might be illegal to ask for fees in your RFP. Instead, we'll look at a fundamental problem that can arise when you ask for architectural fees up front.

When you take bids for the construction of a building, the contractors have the use of a detailed, comprehensive set of drawings and specifications that gives them the exact scope of work that they are to perform. With the information presented to them, they can put together a price that will be profitable for them as well as competitive with the prices of the other contractors bidding on the work.

As soon as fees are requested in a request for proposal, you can find yourself in the same boat with the unnamed municipality whose RFP we discussed earlier in this chapter. Unless you are very specific about the extent of services being requested and can give detailed information regarding the project, the architects will always be somewhat in the dark about the number of hours that it will take them to do the work. There will also be a degree of uncertainty regarding the expectations of the client.

Library boards and library directors are often inexperienced in the selection and hiring of professional consultants. The size of the professional fee is one number that they can pick out of a proposal and really understand. Unfortunately, while they may understand the fee number, they often do not fully understand the services that they are purchasing. Careful study and a well-written RFP are your best preparation. Qualifications-based selection, which we shall be looking at shortly, provides a method for selecting professional services that is more sophisticated than merely looking for the lowest fee.

STEP 4.   FINDING ARCHITECTS

This is the easy part. Even if the local architects haven't already gotten wind of your building plans by the time that you are writing your RFP, it will not usually take a lot of effort on your part to stimulate interest in your project.

Though your office manager might be taking constant telephone calls from would-be applicants, you may still be required to advertise the fact that you are searching for an architect. Laws regulating if, and how, you must advertise your project will differ from one state to another. Consult the library's attorney if you are unsure of the requirements in your case. The requirement is often satisfied by running the advertisement in a local paper of some stated minimum circulation.

An additional way of finding interested architects is to turn to the file in which you place the marketing materials that they and other consultants regularly send the library. Many libraries have a continuously updated file in which these materials are kept on hand for a year and then discarded. If you have this kind of system, the notice that an RFP is available is often sent to all the architects who have materials currently on-file. In some jurisdictions, you are legally required to send the materials to anybody who has a letter of interest in your files.

The devil you know

If the library has successfully used a particular architectural firm in the past, that firm should be a candidate whether or not it currently had materials on-file. Depending upon local statutes, you might not even be required to formally evaluate different architects if you already have a satisfactory, ongoing relationship with a particular firm. If the project that you envisage is much larger or radically different than those that the previous architect has done for you, you still might want to consider a formal interview process with that architect to determine if he or she is capable of the work and to verify that you feel comfortable with the selection.

If all else fails

In the unlikely event that you are having trouble finding architects to contact, there are a few other possible sources for some names

Local libraries: Look around for other libraries that have recently completed construction projects. They will be a good source for both names of architects and reviews of their performance.

System and state libraries: Some will maintain directories of consultants (including architects) that have been used by member libraries.

The directories may also contain information regarding the quality of the services rendered.

The library building consultant: If you are using one, the library building consultant will probably be able to recommend several architectural firms based upon his or her experience with previous projects.

Local offices of the AIA: The American Institute of Architects can be a valuable resource to anyone looking for architectural services. Most branches will publish a directory of architects within their regions along with synopses of the specialties of the listed firms. As an impartial organization, the AIA can offer no opinions regarding the performance of the listed architects.

Limiting the field

Thoroughly evaluating a stack of proposals can be a daunting task. Some libraries in populous areas decide to limit the number of architects being considered to save themselves from having to divide their attention between too many proposals. There are several "filters" that are commonly used. The first is locality. You can often limit the firms under consideration to those within a certain geographic area, the concept being that local firms will be able to offer quicker and more complete service—especially during the construction phase. Another potential advantage is political. If you are trying to pass a referendum, having a local firm may be more "politically correct." They may also be more effective in swaying public opinion. This strategy assumes that the local pool of architects is big enough to offer a sufficient number of firms for comparison. The second most common limiting criterion is setting a minimum limit on the firm's experience in designing libraries. I do not advise this way of limiting your field, as you will be arbitrarily cutting out a number of firms that could provide you with an interesting and successful building.

In the interest of fairness, it is better to publicly limit the field in the request for proposal. This may or may not be possible in your state. The most radical form of limiting the field would be allowing proposals by invitation only, in which a short list of architects is developed, and then the RFPs sent to only those firms. All in all, careful consideration must be given to the concept of limiting the number of architects that you will consider. First, you must ask yourself whether it is legal, and second, are we only doing this to save the building committee some work, or are we convinced that this will promote the public good? Your attorney will be able to answer the first question, the other may require some discussion among the board.

STEP 5.   THE INTERVIEW

It is better to know some of the questions than all of the answers. **James Thurber**

What to do before the interview

Interviews can be the most intense and interesting part of your search for an architect. There are two overriding considerations that you should keep in mind. The first is to make good use of your time with the architects. Do your preparation and have your questions ready. The architect may be writing some of the script, but you are directing the show. It is up to you to insure that things will run smoothly and that everyone will get a fair chance. The second consideration is consistency, make sure that the same questions are asked and the same format followed for each interview. Without this control, a meaningful comparison will be impossible. This is not to say that the whole procedure should be so rigid that the architect is not allowed any outlet for self expression during the interview. Set aside a defined amount of time for each architect to use as he or she sees fit.

Arrive at the short list

The important word here is "short." For most projects, three or four firms should be enough to give you a good cross-section of the types of architects that you are seeking. To generate the short list, the building committee should examine each proposal. Some committees find it useful to rank each one of the respondents using a point system. I recommend that each member of the committee prepare a sort of "secret ballot" in which each firm is rated according to certain, predetermined criteria. The points can then be totaled and the top-ranking three or four firms selected for the short list. I like the secret ballot approach because it helps you get the committee members' true opinions without any undue influence of peer pressure from assertive fellow committee members.

If you use a point system, the categories in which you will rate each architect should be standardized and reflect the priorities of the board. If you are building an addition, you may wish to have one of the ratings reflect the quality of previous additions that the architect lists on the proposal. If your project involves a large degree of site planning, one of the ratings might reflect your desire for a firm that has demonstrated an ability in this area. When deciding on facets of the architectural firms that you wish to rate, it is important that they be coordinated with the request for proposal to insure that the RFP has questions covering the appropriate material. References should also be taken into account while short listing. I suggest that the same person or team contact the references to insure that this process is also standardized. A script of questions should be developed by the selection committee and used for each contact.

Let's assume that you have used a point system and come up with a short list of four firms that you want to consider. There are still a few things to do before the interview.

Inform the applicants

Inform everyone who submitted a proposal whether or not they have made the short list. At this stage, letters will usually suffice. The firms that will be moving on to the interviews should be given a schedule for the interview. Also indicate the format for the interview as well as any other items that will be required by the selection committee.

Check the references

Depending on the number of applicants, you can follow up on references before or after you have formulated the short list. Standardization is again important. Generate of list of questions and run through them with each reference. After asking all your set questions, ask the reference if there is anything else that he or she would like to add. Keeping good notes is very important. If you are visiting the references in person, it might be a good idea to have two members of the selection committee go along so they can compare notes afterward.

In chapter eleven, we looked at a list that could help you evaluate the service that your architect gives you. When put to the architect's references, these same questions can help you evaluate the service that the architect has given other clients. The list can be used as a starting point. Modify it as appropriate for your circumstances.

1. *Did the architect provide all the services that were specified in the contract?*

2. *During the programming phase, was the data efficiently collected and were the program requirements met in the end product?*

3. *Did the architect make appropriate use of materials provided by the library building consultant (if any)?*

4. *Was the architect responsive when you had questions or needed clarifications?*

5. *Was the architect willing to modify the design when requested to do so by the board?*

6. *Was the building produced on budget and in time?*

7. *Did change orders during construction increase the cost of the building by a significant amount?*

8. *Did the architect provide a leadership role in the design and building process?*

9. *Were the architect's budget estimates realistic?*

10. *Were the architect's estimates of the time required for construction realistic?*

11. *Did the architect adequately represent the library in negotiations with civil and municipal authorities?*

12. *Did the architect adequately represent the library in dealings with the contractor?*

13. *Was the architect easy to work with? Did he or she give due attention to your needs?*

14. *Was the total of the professional fees paid to the architect consistent with what you were led to expect?*

15. *Do you feel that you received good value for the money that you spent for professional services?*

16. *Is the building, considering necessary compromises, what you wanted?*

17. *Would you use this architect again?*

When interviewing the architect's references, ask how long ago the services were provided to the references. If any are more than five years old, ask the architect if the same personnel who provided the original services still work in the architect's office. Some offices have a relatively high turnover rate and may bear little resemblance to the offices that they were five or ten years ago.

Decide on a format for the interviews

Deciding on a format for the interviews should be relatively straightforward. Interviews should be kept short, simple and to the point. A sample format might contain the following;

Introductions: Introduce the members of the board and ask the architect to briefly introduce the members of his or her team. The entire design team may not be represented at the interview, but it is important that the person that the architect proposes to use as the project manager for your project be there. When scheduling the interview, make sure to tell the architect to bring the project manager. It is important that you meet the project manager, as this person will be your primary contact with the architect

Questions from the board: Develop a standard set of questions that will be put to each architect. Other questions may come up during the interview as a result of the architect's responses, but make sure to cover the entire list of predetermined questions. Some of the questions may be the same ones on the request for proposal, while others may be for the oral interview only. You may wish to send the architects the list of questions beforehand. It's up to you, but keep in mind that this is not a contest to determine who is best at "thinking on their feet." You are looking for quality rather than for quickness. Some suggested questions will be offered shortly.

Architect's presentation: Allow the architect a predefined amount of time to present whatever he or she thinks is appropriate. To keep things fair, designate someone to watch the clock to insure that the time limit is kept. You will get a wide variety of presentations depending on the size and resources of the firms represented. One firm may show slides of previous work, while another may show renderings, and another might dazzle you with a computer-generated "walk" through their conception of your building.

Try not to be too swayed by impressive presentation styles. A small firm which does high quality work might not have the resources to dedicate the time required to put together a computerized tour of a proposed building. Your task is to look at the message, not the medium.

Final questions from the board: Use this time to ask any additional questions that were inspired by the architect's presentation.

Board discussion: Take a few minutes after the interview to sum up your impressions of the architect and his or her presentation. Make careful notes for later review.

Getting to know you

Deciding what to ask the architect during the questions segment of the interview can be difficult. Start with your request for proposal. Scan the RFP for any questions that need elaboration upon during the oral presentation and include them in your script for the interview. Here are some suggestions for additional material that you might want to cover.

1. *How is the architect's in-house organization set up?*

2. *Who will be the point of contact with the library?*

3. *Does the architect have a design philosophy?*

4. *If so, how does he or she reconcile the design philosophy with the client's wishes when the two come into conflict?*

5. *How does the architect plan to approach this project?*

6. *What does the architect feel is particularly interesting about this project*

7. *What are the principal challenges and opportunities?*

8. *Describe the process you intend to use in designing the building.*

9. *Explain the services that you plan to provide, giving emphasis to the construction and postconstruction phases.*

    (The variations in different architect's services often appear in the latter stages of the project.)

10. *What services can you offer to help us pass the referendum?*

    (This is a legitimate question to ask your architect. Be careful, however, not to get involved in a bidding war to see who will offer the most "free" services. Few services are "free." You will usually pay the bill somewhere else - usually with a higher architectural fee or a reduced scope of services elsewhere.)

11. *If cost overruns or schedule problems on previous projects were apparent during your interviews with the architect's references, give him or her a chance to explain the reasons.*

12. *How does the architect's firm establish its fees?*

    (Don't get into the numbers yet, just find out the architect's standard method for arriving at a fee. Ask how the architect handles fee adjustments due to change orders or projects where the bids come in dramatically higher or lower than the architect estimated.)

13. *Ask the architect what is unique about his or her firm that makes it the most qualified to do the work.*

14. *What will the architect need from the library?*

And on with the show

With your list of questions and format for the interviews completed, you are ready to begin the interviews. Schedule the interviews for nights other than those set aside for the regular board meetings to avoid having to conduct marathon sessions. Allow from 60 to 90 minutes for each architect. If you are interviewing more than two architects, schedule two per session and schedule the sessions for consecutive nights if possible. Two to three hours of interviewing is more than enough for a single night. Remember that there will be additional time required for the board to discuss the interviews and reach some conclusions. As an architect, nothing is more disheartening than to arrive at an interview and see the glazed looks of board members who have just interviewed two or three other firms and are sneaking glances at their watches before you've even begun.

To expedite the process, ask the architects if they will require any special facilities for their presentations and have everything ready to go before the interviews so you won't spend valuable time searching for projection screens or extension cords.

Keep orderly notes of the proceedings and jot down additional comments that occur to you during the board discussions between the interviews. Clients sometimes make audio or video tapes of the interviews to aid them in discussions and evaluations that follow the interviews. This is permissible as long as the applicants are advised beforehand that the proceedings are to be taped. Recording the session is not a substitute for note-taking. My own experience is that a well-written set of notes will usually offer a better summary of what transpired than will an hour's worth of video tape.

STEP 6.   SELECT THE ARCHITECT

When it comes time to make your selection, the first thing that the board will have to do is to decide what the group feels are the most important qualities that they want in their architect. Some of the desired qualities may become apparent to you only after the interview. They might include some of the following:

1. *The quality of the architect's designs*

2. *The architect's experience in designing buildings of a similar size and use.*

3. *The responses of the architect's references.*

4. *Your impressions of the architect's work during visits to previous projects.*

5. *The size of the architect's office vs. the size of your project.*

6. *The "chemistry" between the players and your comfort level with the principal of the firm and with the project manager.*

7. *The architect's understanding of your situation and needs.*

8. *The architect's value to the library for non-design issues like political connections.*

What are you looking for?

The kind of architectural firm that you want to do your work is another consideration. Different kinds of firms will have different strengths. David Maister, a former professor at the Harvard Business School, has defined several generic types of professional firms.[1] The architects you interview can often be characterized by using his categories. Examining firms in this way can help you to identify traits that you wish to have in your architect.

Brains (expertise) firms: These firms are the high design, high profile, high price establishments whose names get a lot of press. They begin their projects with a strong concept and express it throughout the design. The one that you might be looking at might not have designed a lot of libraries, but they are accustomed to tacking new building types. If you want a building with real pizzazz, this is your firm.

Grey hair (experience) firms: A "grey hair" firm might be characterized as one that has designed numerous libraries and has developed a formula designed to insure a successful result time after time. You will not have to spend much of your time teaching them how a library works. On the other hand, you may get a library that is somewhat an "off the shelf" design that has been modified to fit your needs.

Procedure (execution) firms: A "nuts and bolts" outfit. These firms specialize in turning out buildings. They are quick, efficient, relatively low cost and generally not as design-oriented. If your building must go out to bid in six months, this may be the kind of firm to select.

An architectural firm will not usually fall entirely within one category. It can be interesting to ask the architect where his or her firm falls in this group. They may have to express the answer in terms of percentages for each kind of firm, i.e., "50 percent experience and 50 percent execution." Having architects describe their practices in this way can give you insights into how they feel about their businesses, and how they go about serving their clients.

When the interviews are complete and the selection committee has decided upon the priorities, it's time to make your selection. The method that I am going to describe is called "qualifications-based selection", or QBS for short. The first step in QBS is to assign point values that express how each architect satisfies each of the group's chosen criteria. The list of criteria could be drawn from the previously cited eight-point list of items asked during the interview and questions asked of the architect's references. Each member of the board or selection committee individually ranks each architect in each category.

Thus, you might give architect #1 four points out of five for the quality of her designs, five points out of five for the responses of her references and two out of five for her previous experience in library work. This will continue for each criterion. Afterwards, the point values for each architect are totaled and the architects are ranked from most desired to least desired according to their cumulative scores. The advantage of the scoring system is that it takes some of the subjectivity out of the process. An architect with a score of 50 is definitely more highly rated than one with a score of 45. So far it's been (relatively) simple—you've figured out which architect the board likes best. Now is when QBS differs from more traditional methods of selecting professional services.

Qualifications-based selection - QBS

Many states have adopted one form or another of qualifications-based selection. QBS typically regulates the selection and procurement by public bodies of architectural, engineering and land surveying firms. The QBS language used by most states is derived from federal legislation, Public Law 92-582, otherwise known as the Brooks Act. The exact language used in your state, if it is one that has adopted QBS, will have to be reviewed by the library's attorney. Because the method described in the Brooks Act is thorough and systematic, I would propose that your library adopt QBS procedures for hiring architects and engineers even if your state does not require you to do so.

In most states, QBS requires you to take many of the steps that we have already discussed; advertising for firms, accepting proposals, generating a short list of at least three firms, interviewing firms and negotiating with the architects. One important feature has been omitted from this list, and this facet of QBS is what makes it unique.

Until now, fees for professional services have been noticeably absent from our discussions. The true purpose of qualifications-based selection is to insure that professionals hired to do work for public bodies are selected primarily on the basis of their qualifications and only secondarily by their fees. Using the QBS method, the public body begins contract negotiations with the top-rated architect. Indeed, discussing fees is prohibited during the initial selection process. If a price for the his or her services is

agreed upon, that's the end of the procedure. You can sign the contract and begin the project. If you cannot settle upon a price, you can then begin contract negotiations with the architect with the next highest rating. Here's the rub— once you move on to the second architect, you cannot resume negotiations with the first. If you cannot settle with the second architect, you have to go on to the third and are prohibited from resuming negotiations with either of the first two. This process continues either until you settle on a fee with an architect, or until you run out of contestants. If you run out, you would have to begin the entire process again, beginning with advertising your RFP. That is a powerful incentive to settle on a fee with someone in the first group.

You get what you pay for

I warned you that we would eventually come back to this. It could equally be said that you seldom get what you don't pay for. As you may have realized from the above discussion, the intent of the Brooks Act is to insure that public agencies select according to quality rather than by price alone. Most architects do not have a lot of "cushion" built into their fees. The Brooks Act prevents public agencies from using one architect's fee as a lever to bargain down the fee of another. The wisdom of the law is that its authors recognized that when you bargain down a fee, you are also likely to be bargaining away some of the scope of the services that you might have otherwise received. For public work, it was judged that the overall quality and completeness of the work was more important to the public safety than was the apparent savings of a relatively small amount in professional fees.

If you are accountable for spending the public's money, you will no doubt understand a dilemma that is inherent in hiring a professional. You want quality work, but in these tight times, how can you explain to the taxpayers that you didn't hire the lowest "bidder." You realize that you might be leaving yourself open to charges of favoritism or other irregularities. Using QBS, the architect's qualifications rather than the architect's fees become the basis of the "bids" and all negotiations follow a set procedure. If the fees seem excessive, you can always move on to another candidate. Thus, competitive pressures are still brought to bear on the architects as they put together their fees.

A question of self interest

Unfortunately, board members and other public servants have to protect themselves from incurring liability. Whether or not you choose to follow a qualifications-based-selection process, it is incumbent on you to insure that your selection will promote the public's health, safety and welfare. If the library board fails to select an architect or engineer for a project without basing the selection on his or her qualifications, and there was a collapse or other failure that resulted in injury or death, the board could potentially be found negligent. Based on the potential risks, selection established by price alone may not be in either the taxpayers' or your own best interest.

STEP 7. NEGOTIATING WITH THE ARCHITECT

Nothing astonishes men so much as common sense and plain dealing. **Emerson**

The interviews are completed, and the architects have been rated according to the board's preferences and informed of the results. You are ready to sit down and hammer out a deal for the professional services with the top-rated firm. Where do you start? Before you begin, it may pay to do some homework regarding the different ways in which an architect can deliver his or her services and try to formulate some ideas regarding which method best suits your needs. Because most publicly owned organizations must follow the traditional design/award/bid approach, I'm going to emphasize that method. We will touch on the alternatives, however, for those organizations that are able to use them.

Methods of delivery of architectural services

Design/Award/Bid: In this method, the owner signs separate contracts for design and construction. The architect is selected first and prepares the construction documents which are then competitively bid and a qualified contractor is selected based on the amount of the bid.

Advantages:

1. The architect is selected by competitive selection.

2. The architect is the agent of the owner and is employed to act in the best interest of the library.allowing the owner to exercise a greater degree of control over the design and bidding process.

3. Mandated by many state governments for public work.

Disadvantages

1. The final cost of the project is not known until the bids have been received.

2. The contractor is a vendor, supplying a specified product for a set price and acting in his or her own interest.

3. Not as expeditious as fast-track construction.

Fast-track construction with separate contracts for design and construction: For fast-track construction, the prime, or major contractor is selected before the architectural documents are completed. This allows work to begin on some parts of the project while the architect is still completing others. The prime contractor will have many smaller bid openings for different aspects of the project as the architect completes the drawings.

Advantages	Disadvantages
Fast-tracking can speed up the process to help keep to a tight construction schedule.	Requires expert management to accomplish cost containment and time savings.
With more frequent bid openings broken up into smaller portions, greater control of the final cost is possible as it can be tracked on an incremental basis	The greater number of bid openings requires more administrative time by the architect and the owner.
The owner is not "locked into" particular subcontractors for the duration of the project. The sequential bidding process insures that each portion of the work goes to the contractor with the lowest price for that portion of the work.	Many of the project details are not worked out before construction begins. Because of this the number of change orders and the frequency of cost overruns will usually be greater than with a normal project.
The owner has to sign-off on the design on an incremental basis as it progresses. This can reduce the owner's flexibility regarding changes in the design as portions of it may already be under construction while the remainder is "on the drawing board".	Fast-tracking may not be permitted for public projects in your state due to the fact that the initial selection of the prime contractor is not made by competitive bidding.

Design/Build, with or without fast-tracking:
In the design/build format, the architect and the contractor are a single entity. The owner hires a design/build company which produces the drawings and builds the project. If desired, the design/build firm can offer a "guaranteed maximum price" early in the project to facilitate the owner's financing. The design/build company often acts as a broker and bids out many parts of the project as in the case of fast-track construction.

Advantages	Disadvantages
The owner has a single point of responsibility for the design and the construction of the project. There are fewer contracts for the owner to administer.	The architect works for the design/build company, not directly for the owner. Thus, the architect is no longer the agent of the owner.
The design/build firm can offer a guaranteed maximum price relatively early in the project.	The owner must understand that in order to keep to the "guaranteed maximum price," the design/build firm has a certain degree of latitude to adjust aspects of the design to keep the prices under control.
The contractor is involved in all aspects of the design process and can influence the design in order to control costs.	The owner's input in the design process is not as great as with the more traditional methods of building.
Fast-tracking, if required, can speed up the process to help keep to a tight construction schedule.	Design/build is not usually permitted for public work.

Across the table

Once you decide on which services you think that you'll need from your architect, and have an idea of the best way in which those services should be presented you are ready to sit down and begin working out the details of the owner/architect agreement.

The architect will often propose using one of the standard AIA agreements. There are a number of different AIA contracts from which to choose. The appropriate contract will depend on your particular circumstances. Beyond the

"Standard Form Of Agreement Between Owner And Architect," otherwise known as contract B141, there are specialized contracts for designated services, interior design services, projects of limited scope, services performed when the owner is using a construction manager and others. The chances are that the architect will propose using B141 as the basis of your agreement. The use of B141 will be assumed in this discussion.

Unless you have a pressing reason to do otherwise, I suggest that you stick to the standard AIA contracts. Although the contracts were written on behalf of architects, they do a good job at maintaining impartiality with respect to both the architect and the owner. The standard contracts have been developed over many years and cover most of the issues that are likely to come up between the owner and the architect. Some large corporations and public bodies have their own, custom contracts. I advise that you steer away from writing your own unless your attorney has particular experience in this field and has a good background in construction law. As with all contracts, your attorney should review the one that the architect will present to the library. At this time, the attorney can suggest additions or alterations to the standard language that he or she feels are in the best interest of the library.

The first step in the process is to sit down with the architect for a general discussion of the project and your expectations of what services you want the architect to provide. The list of required services that you generated earlier will be your starting point. As a part of the discussions, the architect may suggest modifying your list based on his or her understanding of the project. A good goal for this first meeting might is to arrive at an agreement with the architect concerning the scope of services that will be provided to the library. Direct the architect to prepare a proposal for services and a draft contract for review by library board, the director and the library's attorney. Ask the architect to send you this material before the next meeting so you will have time to review it and formulate your questions. If the architect desires, the fee portion could be left blank until it can be discussed at the next meeting. If the negotiations are being undertaken by a construction committee, be sure that the material is reviewed and approved by the entire board before proceeding.

Before you sign on the dotted line

Before the next meeting with the architect, photocopy the architect's proposal and the preliminary contract so everyone has a copy. The library director and perhaps a board member should read through both of them, line by line. AIA B141, the Standard Form of Agreement Between Owner and Architect, is divided into twelve articles. Pause after each one for questions and discussion. It amounts to about ten pages of text, so you can expect to be at it for some time. I think that this is an important session. Someone other than the library's attorney should have a thorough understanding of the commitments that the library is making by signing the contract, as well as an overview of the range of the architect's responsibilities.

Article 3 itemizes additional services by the architect and also deserves scrutiny. Remember that programming, extensive on-site representation during construction and postconstruction services are not a part of the "basic services" of the architect's contract. Article 3 must be customized to cover the services that you and the architect have decided should be included. The cost for these additional services will be broken out as separate line items in the part of the contract where the architect gives the fee.

Pay special attention to Article 4 which outlines the owner's responsibilities. Many of the things that you are agreeing to will cost the library money to provide. These costs should be evaluated and considered when you are putting together the project budget. It's important that you realize that the project budget will be larger than the construction budget. Items like the ones listed in Article 4 will add to your total cost. The architect should be able to assist you in estimating many of these additional expenses.

Your attorney may have suggested some changes to the standard contract. Article 7, mandates arbitration as the means of settling claims or disputes relating to the architectural agreement. This section is often deleted or modified by the library's lawyer (with lawyers, arbitration is not a popular method of resolving disputes). Discuss all proposed alterations to the contract to insure that everyone is agreed. A single, master copy of the contract could be marked up during the session and then photocopied so everyone has a record of the agreement.

One last item of particular interest is the architect's reimbursable expenses which are defined in Article 10 of the contract. Postage, phone calls, printing, computer-aided drafting, renderings and models are among the items that will be discussed here. In addition to agreeing on which items will be included as reimbursables, you should discuss what forms of documentation you will require from the architect to substantiate claims for reimbursement. Some things like expenses for reproductions and long distance phone calls are relatively easy as the architect can provide receipts and phone bills as back-up. For others, like the costs of drawing renderings and building models, you may have to rely on the architect's records of hours spent on the task. Whenever possible, try to get the architect to agree to a maximum cost for those kinds of services. Because of uncertainty regarding the scope of these additional services the architect may not be willing to commit to a cost until later in the project when the scope will be better defined.

The bottom line

The last step in negotiating with your architect is agreeing on a fee. There are several ways that an architect can put together a fee for the project. We'll look at the most common arrangements.

The fee as a stipulated sum. In this arrangement, the architect sets the fee based on his or her determination of the value of the services to be provided. The fee will usually be based on the architect's estimate of the projected number of hours and other expenses that will be required to complete the project. An advantage of this method is that the owner and the architect know what the fees will be before the project begins. Should the scope of the project increase after the owner/architect agreement is signed, the architect's fee will be adjusted upward in proportion to the change. When another method is used to determine the architect's fee for the basic services, stipulated sums are often used to define costs for any additional services

The fee as a percentage of the construction cost. This is another common arrangement. It assumes that the larger the job, the more time it will take the architect to design, draw and coordinate the project. In addition, the architect's exposure to liability increases as the size of the project increases. The assumption that difficulty parallels project size is sometimes borne out, sometimes not. The final fee cannot be calculated until the project is bid and built. Because of this, the early payments to the architect will be based upon the estimated cost of the project with adjustments being made later as the cost of the project is determined. Exactly what is included in the "construction cost" must be clearly defined beforehand.

Cost-plus fee. This type of fee is based upon the direct costs to the architect times a predetermined multiplier. There are a number of variations:

Multiple of the architect's direct salary expenses. This is a multiple of the architect's payroll.

Multiple of the architect's direct personnel expense. This includes the fringe benefits of the staff in the equation.

Professional fee plus expenses. This begins with a "professional fee" to which the architect's expenses are added.

Hourly. This is usually based on a predetermined billing rate for each employee. The rates should be agreed upon before the contract is signed.

The major disadvantage of cost-plus-fee arrangements is that the owner might not have any idea of what the total fee will be. If you are considering this type of arrangement, I recommend that you ask the architect to give you a "cost not to exceed" figure that will fix the maximum amount that the library could be billed.

Cost-plus-fees are most suited to projects of limited duration where the scope of the work has not been fully established, they are often used for initial feasibility studies. They are often prohibited for publicly- funded projects because of the uncertainty of the magnitude of the fee.

How much?

Professional ethics forbid architects from any actions that could be interpreted as "price fixing," so I cannot give you examples of fees for particular types of projects. In any case, it would be meaningless to do so as each project has its own set of circumstances that will influence the amount of the architect's fee.

There are some general rules that will apply to most projects. The first is that the fee should reflect the difficulty of the project. Looked at as a percentage of the project cost, the architect's fee for designing a warehouse would be relatively less than the fee for designing a hospital, or a library. The second general rule is that fees will be relatively higher for smaller projects. The fee that an architect would have to charge to design a new circulation desk for a library would probably be a higher percentage of the project cost than the fee for designing a new library. The circulation desk will, of course, be a much smaller project with perhaps only one sheet of details compared to twenty or more architectural sheets for an entire building. Similarly, the fee as a percentage for designing a 70,000 square foot library would usually be less than the percentage for designing a similar library of 20,000 square feet. The third general rule is that projects with special requirements, like abbreviated or lengthy schedules, will generally cost more as the architect must make up for overtime pay in the first case or, in the second case, for the greater number of hours that will be expended in doing the project.

Sticker shock

In the discussion on construction documents I gave some examples of the amount of time that it takes an architect to produce a set of working drawings. You may remember that I said that some offices assume 40 to 60 hours of time will be spent on each sheet of drawings. Assuming a medium-sized project of twelve or so sheets, take twelve sheets times 40 hours per sheet and you arrive at an estimated 480 to 720 hours of drawing time. Multiply the hours by the billing rate for the architect's staff of 40 by $50 or more per hour and you wind up with some significant cost numbers. On top of this, consider that time spent by the project manager or the principal will usually be billed out at a higher rate and that the construction documents portion of the project might only represent something like 40% of the architect's total fee.

Unless you are accustomed to dealing with fees for professional services, the numbers that are generated in the above analysis can be surprising. More than once, I've seen a client's jaw drop when they heard the proposed fee for a project. Things usually settle down when we explain how we arrived at the fee, but there can be a few uncomfortable moments for everybody until the explanation is understood.

As one of the people responsible for selecting the architect, the "sticker shock" syndrome can present you with a problem. You may, at first, be shocked by the fee. You began the negotiation process with the firm that you want to do the work. Do you accept this fee or move on to another architect? An alternative to moving on to the next architect is to negotiate with the first architect for a lower fee. Sometimes the architect will have started with a "rock bottom" fee and will be unwilling to go any lower, while at other times there may be some room for negotiation.

How do you know it's fair?

There's nothing wrong with asking the architect for some backup information that will show you how he or she established the fee. Sometimes it's less of an issue of affordability than one of you being able to justify the expense to the taxpayers or whoever else is in control of the project funding. In this case, the backup information supplied by the architect can give you some of the justification that you need. Going back to your discussions with the architect's references is another approach. If most of them feel that they received good value for the money that they spent on professional fees, you will have an added reason for negotiating with this architect rather than going on to your second choice.

In the final analysis, you have to satisfy yourself that you have arrived at an equitable fee arrangement. When the board is comfortable with the amount, you can sit down and sign the contract. Hiring an architect can take a surprising amount of your time. If you give it the attention that it deserves and use some of the methods that I've outlined for you, chances are that you will have no reason to regret your decision.

In Conclusion: The Great Circle Route

We shall not cease from exploration
And the end of all our exploring
Will be to arrive where we started
And know the place for the first time
T. S. Eliot

We have come full-circle. We began by talking about architects and what they do. Next, we looked at the parts of a typical architectural project and at how they might apply to your situation. In the end, we returned to architects and looked at how you might find and hire one. Throughout all of this, there has been one, prime purpose. The aim has been to help you build a better library. An architect is one of the many tools that you will use to accomplish your goal. Knowing the right tool for the job and how to use it is a good first step for any project.

I hope that this book will be of use to you. Our society is changing rapidly and the role of the library within it is changing as well. It remains to be seen how the library's role will evolve. In fact, the only thing that we know for sure is that the library will evolve, must evolve to keep pace with the growing technology of the electronic transfer of information. Within the space of a decade or two, the workings of libraries will advance from nineteenth century technology to that of the twenty-first century. This evolution will require that new libraries be built and existing ones adapted to enable them to take on these new roles. It is the partnership between library boards, library professionals and architects that will help make possible the birth of this new kind of library.

I welcome your questions and comments regarding this book, please feel free to send them to me via the publisher and I will try to incorporate them into any future editions. I wish you good luck in your building endeavors.

Notes

1. David Maister. *Managing the Professional Service Firm.* New York: Free Press, 1994.

Appendix I: Request for Proposal

ROOSEVELT LIBRARY DISTRICT

REQUEST FOR PROPOSAL
FOR
ARCHITECTURAL SERVICES

The Roosevelt Library District is seeking specific qualifications from interested architectural firms that are capable of providing professional services for the siting, design and construction of a new library. The library district serves a population of 90,000 and is currently located in a 45,000 square foot building located at 429 Augusta Avenue, Ourtown. Based upon the recommendations of the library building consultant, it is anticipated that the new library shall be approximately 70,000 square feet in area.

I. Description of the Architect Procurement Process

The process for procurement of Architect services will proceed in two stages.

A. Submission of Written Qualifications

The Library Board will review and evaluate the written responses to the Request for Proposal (RFP) in accordance with the evaluation criteria identified in Attachment "A" The Library Board will select no more than three qualified architects to proceed to the competitive oral interview stage of the procurement process.

(Limit the number of firms to be interviewed to no more than three or four at the most.)

B. Oral Interview

Each of the selected qualified architects will participate in a detailed oral interview to more fully discuss how their approach to this project satisfies the evaluation criteria set forth in Attachment A. In addition, architects will be required to answer questions posed by the Selection Committee. It will be the sole responsibility of the Selection Committee to rank the candidates in order of qualification on the basis of the evaluation of the written responses to the Request for Proposal and oral responses received during the interview process. The top ranking candidate shall then be invited to proceed to the negotiation stage.

(If your state mandates a qualifications-based selection (QBS) approach, you might want to state that the final selection will be based on QBS procedures. See chapter 12 for an overview of Quality-Based Selection.)

II. Site Visits / Facility Tours

The Library Director will be available to answer questions about the proposed site and operation of the present library. All architects are encouraged to carefully evaluate the library data contained in the RFP and visit the potential site(s) as well as the existing facility to enhance their understanding of the project. Please contact the Library Director to schedule site visits.

III. Scope of Services Desired

The professional services of the Architect will be based on Document B141, the standard AIA owner/architect agreement and shall include the following.

(Be sure to state any special requirements that you may have that aren't covered as part of the "basic services" of the standard owner/architect contract. You can obtain copies of the standard contract from the American Institute of Architects, or from a local architectural firm.)

Phase I

A. Site selection criteria / architectural programming / predesign. (The architect's professional fee for this portion of the work shall be negotiated separately.)

    1. Programming shall incorporate and build upon the program produced by the library building consultant.

    2. The library district shall provide the architect with detailed information about the existing site utilities. This will include a boundary survey, topographic information and a phase I environmental analysis.

(Environmental analyses may be required for your project. If you are in doubt, contact your local building authorities. They can tell you where to go for additional information.)

B. Schematic Design and cost estimate.

    1. At the close of the schematic design phase, the architect shall submit a project cost estimate prepared by an independent, professional cost estimator.

(The cost estimate by an independent professional estimator is optional and is by no means standard practice in the industry. In smaller communities, there may be no professional estimators available.)

    2. The architect shall provide a scale model of the proposed library on the site. This model shall be of such quality as to enable it to be displayed to the public during the referendum drive. *(Models are optional and can be costly.)*

    3. The architect shall provide at least two renderings of the proposed library on the site. The renderings shall be mounted on illustration board and be of such quality as to enable them to be displayed to the public during the referendum drive.

C. Referendum services.

    1. Members of the design team who are familiar with the design shall be available to attend at least three public meetings where they will answer public questions regarding the project.

Phase II (Postreferendum services, contingent upon passage of a building referendum)

D. Design Development

    1. At the close of the design development phase, the architect shall submit a project cost estimate prepared by an independent, professional cost estimator.

(See the note following Section B1.)

E. Construction Documents

F. Bidding and Negotiation

G. Construction Phase

Certain items related to the development of the site shall be included in this contract. These items are as follows:

1. An small, story area for children's programs.
2. A nature trail in the oak grove to the north of the proposed library site.

(List design items that are unique to your project or that you feel will enhance the architect's understanding of your wishes.)

IV. Project Size and Individual Characteristics

The complete program for this library has not yet been developed. It is anticipated that this facility will serve as the Library District's main facility. Some of the main components of this facility will be:

A. 20,000± square foot central collection area

B. Staff offices

C. Maintenance supply room

D. Multipurpose rooms for meetings or programs

E. Lobby

F. Circulation desk

G. Mainframe computer room

H. Individual instruction / tutoring rooms

I. Board meeting room

J. Seating for 400 patrons

K. Children's library

L. Youth library

Detailed information regarding programming requirements for library services is contained in the report submitted by the library building consultant. Copies of this report are available for $30 each (Nonrefundable). Contact the library director to obtain copies of the report.

The facility shall meet all the requirements of the Americans With Disabilities Act.

ATTACHMENT A
EVALUATION CRITERIA

The following criteria will be used to evaluate the written submissions of each architect's qualifications. The comments of the architect's previous clients of the architect will also be considered. (These are not ranked in order of importance).

A. Project Management

1. There shall be a clear assignment of responsibilities for various project tasks to specific individuals. All individuals with major responsibilities for the project's design, bidding specification and follow-through should be identified at the oral interview.
2. The architect shall have a demonstrated ability to observe construction, and handle field changes and other contingencies that may arise during construction.
3. The architect shall be able to demonstrate that he/she has provided effective management, design and monitoring services on past projects.
4. The architect shall demonstrate an ability to complete projects within budget and according to schedule.
5. The architect's responsiveness to the specific user goals identified in the RFP.
6. The quality of communication skills and the effectiveness of the project manager and on-site construction representative from your firm.
7. The ability to coordinate project construction with contractors, equipment suppliers and Library District personnel.

B. Technical Approach - The following items will be considered

1. The architect shall exhibit an understanding of the existing conditions, systems, operations, and schedules.
2. Qualifications of the design professionals.
3. The number of past projects completed by the architect which are similar to this one in scope or complexity.
4. The quality and performance of architect's past projects. This shall be evaluated by the board during walkthroughs of several of the architects completed buildings and interviews with former clients.

Designing Better Libraries

ATTACHMENT B

REQUEST FOR PROPOSAL TIME LINE

Activity	Date
Issue RFP's	_____
Written Proposals due no later than 1:00 P.M.	_____
Written Proposals evaluated by Library Board.	_____
Three Architecture firms selected for short list and notified of oral interview.	_____
Facility Tours	_____
Oral Interviews (approximately 1 hour each) by Project Evaluation Team	_____
Selection committee's recommendation to the Library Board	_____
Contract negotiations with selected architect	_____
Post-selection requirements	_____

(Fill in dates as appropriate for your project.)

ATTACHMENT C

FIRM PROFILE / PERFORMANCE HISTORY

Applicants must submit responses to the following;

Written material should be sent to the building committee of the Roosevelt Library, 1928 Hoover Place, Ourtown. Submittals must be received before 1:00 p.m., April 1, 1997.

(Keep your requests for information short and specific. Avoid philosophical essay questions. They tend to make the respondents more concerned with trying to tell you what you want to hear instead of sticking to the facts. Lists of required submittals should be concise to insure that you receive similar proposals from each firm.)

A. Outline of Qualifications

Please provide the following information:

1. Firm Name/Address
2. General history of the firm including, but not limited to:
   (a) Number of years in business
   (b) Type of ownership, and name(s) of owners
   (c) Type of organization
   (d) Geographical area of operations
   (e) Professional affiliations
   (f) Amounts and kinds of professional insurance carried
3. Personnel in your present organization
   (a) Who are the principals in your organization?
   (b) What is the size and composition of your organization?
   (c) Please include resumes of personnel that you propose to assign to this project.
4. What types of special consultant services not provided by your firm will the Library need to obtain?
5. What additional consultants would you propose to hire to supplement your firm's basic architectural services? Please provide their names and relevant experience.
6. List any additional related services that your firm can provide, such as interior design, energy management, etc.

B. Past Performance

1. Please indicate up to five similar size buildings that you have designed in the past ten years including location, size, and cost.
2. Indicate what buildings your firm currently has in progress with location, size and cost of each.

(Questions 1 and 2 should not be limited to library buildings. In many ways, you can better evaluate an architectural firm by seeing examples of a number of different types of buildings they have designed.)

3. List the total cost of change orders on each of the above projects.

(This is often asked on RFPs. As they can arise for any number of reasons, the cost of change orders does necessarily have a direct correlation with the quality of the

architect's service. If you ask this question, give the architect an opportunity to discuss the reasons for the change orders.)

    4.   Considering previous commitments you have made for architectural services, can the work on the project be scheduled in your office for immediate participation upon selection as the project architect?

C. Supplemental Information

    1.   Please provide other pertinent information that you feel makes you qualified for the proposed project. Limit supplemental information to one typewritten page.

(Place strict limits on the amount of supplemental information that you will accept. Without limitations, some architects will be brief and concise, while others will overwhelm you with every scrap of information they feel could possibly be to their advantage. These kinds of disparities can make it difficult to compare proposals.)

D. References

    1.   Provide references that may be contacted for each of the projects listed. Include name, title, phone number and address for each contact person.

It is the intent of the library board to tour several buildings designed by each of the potential architectural firms.

(Visits to completed projects can be an important part of the selection process. Try to visit at least one project that is five years old or more to evaluate how buildings designed by the architect are holding up.)

ATTACHMENT D

ANTICIPATED PROJECT TIME LINE

Activity   **Date**

Selection of architectural firm   —————

Notification of architectural firm and beginning of
programming and schematic design   —————

Programming and schematic design complete   —————

Referendum activities begin   —————

Referendum   —————

Building design resumed (contingent upon
passage of referendum)   —————

Building design complete   —————

Bidding   —————

Beginning of construction   —————

Estimated date of substantial completion   —————

*(Make your best guess regarding the project time line. You may only know a few of
the dates with any certainty. Even if you only know the dates of the selection of the
architect and of the referendum, the information will help the architect evaluate
staffing requirements within his or her office. Be sure to specify if you must take
occupancy of the building by a certain date.)*

End of Request For Proposal

Appendix II: Advertisement for Bids

Project Name and Location:
A Library for the Roosevelt Library District
429 August Ave.
Yourtown, Yourstate

Give the official name of your project as well as its location.

Owner:
The Roosevelt Library District.
1928 Hoover Place
Yourtown, Yourstate

Indicate the name of the public body responsible for the project, and the address to which correspondence should be directed.

Architect:
Bussard, Stever and Totes Inc.
2425 Mire Lane
Yourtown, Yourstate
(212) 555-5555

Give the name of the architectural firm responsible for the bidding documents, along with the phone number

Project Description:
This project is to construct a 75,000 square foot, single story library building...(continue as appropriate)

Continue with project specifics as required to briefly summarize the project. Keep it as short as possible to reduce the cost of the advertisement.

Documents:
Bidding documents will be available at the office of the architect after 1:00 p.m., April 1, 1995.

Coordinate this with the architect.

Deposit:
A refundable deposit of $100.00 will be required for each of the first three sets of documents issued to prospective bidders. Additional sets may be purchased for $100.00 each. Unused sets must be returned for refund within thirty calendar days after bidding.

Coordinate these requirements with the architect. Bidding sets cost the architect (and hence the owner) a significant amount of money to reproduce and should not be given away too freely.

Bid Forms:
Each bidder will be required to submit two original, signed copies of the bid forms contained in the bidding package.

Coordinate this with the architect.

Bid Security:
A bid bond in the amount of 10% of the bid amount shall be included with the completed bid forms.

Consult the architect and the library's legal counsel regarding bid security amounts and restrictions.

Bids Due:
Bids are due by 10:00 a.m. prevailing time on April 21, 1995. Bids will be received at the business office located in the library at 1928 Hoover Place, Yourtown, Yourstate.
Late bids will be rejected.

Coordinate this with the architect to help insure that adequate time is being allotted for the bidding process.

Bid Opening:
Bids will be publicly opened at the library business office at 11:00 a.m., prevailing time April 21, 1995.

Bids are usually opened on a weekday during business hours. If your project is sizable, you may need to hold it in a room large enough to accommodate a large number of people who have come to watch the opening.

Prequalification of Bidders:
Bidders will be required to be prequalified. Information regarding the prequalification of bidders is contained in the bid package.

Consult the architect and the library's legal counsel regarding the legalities and desirability of prequalifying bidders.

Bonds:
Performance and labor and material payment bonds will be required in the full amount of the contract sum. Bonds will be made payable to the Roosevelt Library District.

Consult the architect and the library's legal counsel regarding acceptable bond ratings and appropriate bond amounts.

Agreement:
AIA Document A101, Standard Agreement Between Owner and Contractor.

Cite the contract being used. Usually, it will be a standard AIA contract.

Contract Time:
All work under this contract shall be substantially complete by June 1, 1997.

Consult the architect regarding the appropriate construction time for your building. The completion date will be determined by the particulars of your project.

End of Advertisement for Bids

Appendix III: Punch List

Date prepared: July 27, 1996   Date of Inspection: 7/27/96, Page 1 of 2

Contractor: **Project:**

James Enterprises Ltd.   New library for the Roosevelt Library District

50 E. Newer Ave.   429 Augusta Ave.

Yourtown, Yourstate

Contract No. 93-0454-81

Contract Work: General

The following is a list of items to be completed or corrected by the contractor. The failure to include any item on this list does not relieve the contractor of his or her responsibility to complete all work in accordance with the contract documents.

Item No.	Location	Description of Completion or Correction
1.	Lobby (Room#101), door number one	Provide pull on north door.
2.	Lobby (Room#101), door number one	Touch up paint on door and paint exterior and interior door frame.
3.	Lobby (Room#101)	Coats Racks were not installed.
4.	Lobby (Room#101)	Mini Blinds were not installed.
5.	Lobby (Room#101)	The wall angle of the ceiling grid in all the rooms is not flush with the wall, this is causing the tiles to be raised. The angle needs to be adjusted.
6.	Lobby (Room#101)	Repair wood crown above door #1.
7.	Lobby (Room#101)	Install all shelves in the cabinets.
8.	Lobby (Room#101)	Provide flush bolt insert in concrete at north door.
9.	Exhibit Area (Room#102)	Provide flush entry mat. Trim mat to fit in opening.
10.	Exhibit Area (Room#102)	Remove paint on the louver in the ceiling.
11.	Exhibit Area (Room#102)	Repair wood crown mould above door #1.
12.	Exhibit Area (Room#102)	Caulk joint at 45 degree wall were the drywall meets the concrete.
13.	Exhibit Area (Room#102)	Provide entry mat. Trim mat to fit in opening.
14.	Exhibit Area (Room#102)	Remove paint on thermostat.

Prepared by: Reviewed By:

Date Prepared: July 28, 1996

BUSSARD, STEVER & TOTES - ARCHITECTS

Appendix IV: Bibliography

BOOKS

American Institute of Architects. *The Architect's Handbook of Professional Practice*. Washington, DC: AIA, 1993.

American Institute of Architects. *Selecting Architects for Public Projects*. Washington, DC: AIA, 1982. Reprinted 1986.

American Institute of Architects and Consulting Engineers Council of Illinois. *Qualifications-Based Selection*. Chicago: AIA Illinois and CECI Illinois, 1993.

Dahlgren, Anders. *Planning the Small Public Library Building*. Chicago: American Library Association, 1985. No. 11 in the Small Libraries Publications series, this brief 24 page handbook summarizes basic steps in preparing for a building project.

Dailey, Kazuko. *Library Buildings Consultant List*. Chicago: ALA, 1993. Provides the names, addresses, and the special experience offered by library building consultants.

Finn, Richard and James R. Johnston, *Selecting Library Consultants*. Chicago: Illinois Library Association, 1989. (Part of the Trustee Facts File)

Illinois House of Representatives, Illinois Public Act 87-673; An Act Concerning Procurement of Architectural, Engineering, and Land Surveying Services by the State of Illinois. Springfield, IL: State of Illinois, 1987.

Illinois Library Association, Public Library Section. *Avenues to Excellence II, Standards for Public Library Service in Illinois* 1989. Chicago: ILA, 1989.

Palmer, Michey A., *The Architect's Guide to Facility Planning*. The American Institute of Architects and Architectural Record Books. Washington, DC: AIA, 1981.

Peña, William, William Caudill, and John Focke. *Problem Seeking*. New York: Cahners Books International, 1977.

Professional Engineers in Private Practice, *Questions and Answers on the Procurement of A/E Services by Public Owners*. Alexandria, VA: National Society of Professional Engineers, undated.

Thompson, Richard, *Building a New Library*. Chicago: Illinois Library Association, 1989. (Part of the Trustee Facts File)

Articles

Coxe, Weld, et al. "Charting Your Course." *Architectural Technology* (May/June 1986), pp. 52-58.

Kuster, Larry D. and Mann-Stadt, Rendi. "Selecting Professional Services and Local Government Liability." *AIA Illinois News* (Summer, 1993), pp. 2, 11.

Natale, Joe, ed. "Special Construction Considerations." *Illinois Libraries* (December 1991), pp. 617-636.

Index